SpringerBriefs in Economics

AF847527

SpringerBriefs present concise summaries of cutting-edge research and practical applications across a wide spectrum of fields. Featuring compact volumes of 50 to 125 pages, the series covers a range of content from professional to academic. Typical topics might include:

- A timely report of state-of-the art analytical techniques
- A bridge between new research results, as published in journal articles, and a contextual literature review
- A snapshot of a hot or emerging topic
- An in-depth case study or clinical example
- A presentation of core concepts that students must understand in order to make independent contributions

SpringerBriefs in Economics showcase emerging theory, empirical research, and practical application in microeconomics, macroeconomics, economic policy, public finance, econometrics, regional science, and related fields, from a global author community.

Briefs are characterized by fast, global electronic dissemination, standard publishing contracts, standardized manuscript preparation and formatting guidelines, and expedited production schedules.

More information about this series at http://www.springer.com/series/8876

Nina Ismael

Strategic Interaction Between Islamist Terror Groups

A Game Theoretic Approach

Springer

Nina Ismael
BwConsulting
Cologne, Nordrhein-Westfalen, Germany

ISSN 2191-5504 ISSN 2191-5512 (electronic)
SpringerBriefs in Economics
ISBN 978-3-030-51306-1 ISBN 978-3-030-51307-8 (eBook)
https://doi.org/10.1007/978-3-030-51307-8

© The Author(s), under exclusive license to Springer Nature Switzerland AG 2020
This work is subject to copyright. All rights are reserved by the Publisher, whether the whole or part of the material is concerned, specifically the rights of translation, reprinting, reuse of illustrations, recitation, broadcasting, reproduction on microfilms or in any other physical way, and transmission or information storage and retrieval, electronic adaptation, computer software, or by similar or dissimilar methodology now known or hereafter developed.
The use of general descriptive names, registered names, trademarks, service marks, etc. in this publication does not imply, even in the absence of a specific statement, that such names are exempt from the relevant protective laws and regulations and therefore free for general use.
The publisher, the authors, and the editors are safe to assume that the advice and information in this book are believed to be true and accurate at the date of publication. Neither the publisher nor the authors or the editors give a warranty, expressed or implied, with respect to the material contained herein or for any errors or omissions that may have been made. The publisher remains neutral with regard to jurisdictional claims in published maps and institutional affiliations.

This Springer imprint is published by the registered company Springer Nature Switzerland AG.
The registered company address is: Gewerbestrasse 11, 6330 Cham, Switzerland

Acknowledgments

Foremost, I would like to express my sincere gratitude to my supervisor and, more importantly, friend Prof. Dr. Joerg Schimmelpfennig, who did not only provide me with the opportunity to write a doctoral thesis and work at his Chair for Theoretical and Applied Microeconomics but also cared so much about me. Thank you for your continuous support, your patience, and your persistence—in all situations.

I am also grateful to the team behind the scenes. Thank you to Annika, Lucia, and Katja for encouraging and supporting me along the way. I had—and already have—a wonderful time with you.

Finally, I express my gratitude to the people who gave me the opportunities and experiences that have made me who I am—Mark, for his nerves of steel, my father Frank, who had the unbreakable habit to relativize things, and my mother Lioba, who, I am pretty sure, is watching over me, from wherever that may be.

Contents

List of Figures

List of Table

Chapter 1
Introduction

Abstract The coordinated terrorist incidents on the World Trade Center and the Pentagon on September 11th, 2001, (henceforth 9/11) by *al-Qaeda* exhibited the vulnerability of powerful nation-states to jihadist groups. The American response to 9/11 was the now called Global War on Terrorism, which began with the invasion in Afghanistan and the overthrow of the Taliban regime and also led to the American doctrine of preemptive military actions and the invasion of Iraq in 2003.

The coordinated terrorist incidents on the World Trade Center and the Pentagon on September 11th, 2001, (henceforth 9/11) by *al-Qaeda* exhibited the vulnerability of powerful nation-states to jihadist groups. The American response to 9/11 was the now called Global War on Terrorism, which began with the invasion in Afghanistan and the overthrow of the Taliban regime and also led to the American doctrine of preemptive military actions and the invasion of Iraq in 2003.

Since then, jihadism has grown dramatically and the international community, the United States of America foremost, has spent energy and money to counter Islamic terrorism and to defeat *al-Qaeda*. The successful elimination of *al-Qaeda*-leader Osama bin Laden and the devastation of *al-Qaeda*'s core leadership in 2011 led to the conventional wisdom that the terror group was substantially weakened. In the public perception, *al-Qaeda* has sunken into obscurity since 2014, when another terror organization came into international spotlight due to a military blitz, which resulted in the capture of Fallujah, Mosul, and large parts of the Nineveh province, and the declaration of a caliphate. However, the rise of the so-called *Islamic State* (from now on *Daesh*[1]) did not appear out of nowhere. The focus on *al-Qaeda* the years before has blinded, among others, the Obama administration to the growth of *Daesh* and led to an underestimation of its capabilities, not least revealed by Obama, who referred to *Daesh* as a "*JV-team*,"[2] while it seized more and more territory.

[1]The name *Daesh* is the Arabic acronym of *ISIS* and is used in order to undermine the organization's claim to have rebuilt the Caliphate (Irshaid 2015).

[2]A junior varsity (JV) team is a college-team in sports that consists of members, who are not the main players. Players of a "JV-team" are considered to be rookies.

© The Author(s), under exclusive license to Springer Nature Switzerland AG 2020

N. Ismael, *Strategic Interaction Between Islamist Terror Groups*, SpringerBriefs in Economics, https://doi.org/10.1007/978-3-030-51307-8_1

In addition to its territorial successes, *Daesh* became famous for its brutal violence, including torture, crucifixions, and beheadings, exhibited by figures such as "Jihadi John," recorded on video, and distributed through social media channels. *Daesh* managed to attract an unprecedented number of foreign fighters, and in 2014, *Daesh* seemed to have replaced *al-Qaeda* and to dwarf the organization, which was able to conduct 9/11.

Not only since 9/11 social sciences deal with the phenomenon of terrorism, but the events certainly fostered the growth and popularity of terrorism research. Particularly, the realm of economics and game theory became relevant to the study of terrorism. However, research on terrorism has been continually plagued by a discussion on definitions and controversies concerning methods. Furthermore, the nature of terrorism and the heterogeneity of terrorist attacks make empirical investigations inherently difficult. Because terror organizations seem to strike randomly, the descriptive and explanatory power of models dealing with terrorism is continually on trial.

Terrorism research provides two explanations for the occurrence of terrorism. On the one hand, it is argued that terrorism is caused by political, economic, or religious grievances. On the other hand, researchers acknowledge that terrorism is a concept that best ensures an organization's sustainability and longevity. Understanding terror attacks as a method of recruitment and organizational cohesion helps to explain much of the, prima facie, abnormal behavior. A debate on terror incidents that serve the maintenance of a group allows for a consideration of strategic interactions between terror groups in order to explain certain attack patterns, between terror.

Based on the necessity of group survival, Bloom (2004, 2005) argues that terror groups, which compete for adherents, media attention, and funding, will engage in more and more violence to signal their capabilities and commitments to their causes, and thereby "outbid" competitors. Attacks are anticipated to bring support to the most capable terror group, so that the existence of competitors is assumed to incentivize a terrorist group to stage dramatic incidents. Competition, thus, leads to an increase in terrorist attacks, either quantitively or qualitatively.

The "outbidding-hypothesis" is of great intuitive appeal and has become increasingly popular within the field of terrorism research as an explanation for the occurrence of terrorist incidents. However, the idea is fueled merely by anecdotical and some empirical evidence. It still lacks a model-theoretical analysis that captures the attack behavior of similar groups and approaches the implementation of terrorist incidents as a process of strategic interaction.

This thesis seeks to understand the role of competition on the attack behavior of terror organizations by developing a game-theoretical model, which enables the study of strategic interaction among terrorist groups, competing for funding and followers. The analysis will show that a contest between two organizations can be interpreted as a race for support, which, in turn, may explain, why dramatic attacks occur at all, though not as a result of outbidding but as a result of losing the race. Nevertheless, it also reveals that groups vying for superiority among their followership have in incentive to participate in the race and to risk losing instead of choosing an attack pattern that provides them with a better outcome, when compared to the outcome of losing.

Furthermore, arguments are found that competition does not necessarily lead to more attacks but can result in less terrorism due to an increased probability of attack failure induced by the race. This is different from the idea of outbidding, which attributes a reduction of terrorism to a decline in the acceptance of terrorist violence within the followership.

The dissertation is composed as follows: Chap. 2 will provide some general information on terrorism. It shortly introduces into the difficulties of finding a generally accepted definition and explains why some groups engage in terrorism, while others do not. Further, the economic impacts of terrorist incidents are discussed.

Chapter 3 conceptualizes the phenomenon of terrorism. First, some implications of strategy and tactics concerning terrorism are discussed briefly, followed by a comparison to guerrilla warfare. Then, the different concepts of terrorism are presented. The chapter closes with a comment on the choice of target.

Chapter 4 provides an overview of how economic theory can be applied to the analysis of terrorism by starting to examine how to deal with the—to economists—fundamental assumption of rationality in the context of terrorism. The subsequent section will demonstrate how game theory can be used to analyze terrorism. Moreover, different aspects of competition are highlighted.

In Chap. 5, a game-theoretical model is developed in order to understand the effects of competition on terrorist activities. The model, then, is applied to *al-Qaeda*, its unofficial offshoot *Jabhat Fateh al-Sham*, and *Daesh* in Chap. 6. Plausible arguments are found that justify why it is reasonable to believe that *al-Qaeda* will conduct a large-scale event, whereas *Daesh* is forced to conduct small-scale attacks. Chapter 7 concludes and summarizes the results.

References

Bloom MM (2004) Palestinian suicide bombing: Public support, market share, and outbidding. Political Science Quarterly 119(1):61–88

Bloom M (2005) Dying to kill: the allure of suicide terror. Columbia University Press, New York, NY

Irshaid F (2015) Isis, Isil, IS or Daesh? One group, many names. BBC. Accessed 29 Sept 2018. https://www.bbc.com/news/world-middle-east-27994277

Chapter 2
On Terrorism

Abstract Almost a century ago, the international community dealt with fascism. Less than a half-century ago, communism was perceived to be a blister on society. The formation, collapse, and reconstruction of states and the Eastern bloc were related to changes in the way wars were fought and in where and how they were fought. Although terrorism is not a new phenomenon, the recent decades have been marked by an increase in religiously ideological terrorism and Islamist-jihadists manipulating supportive civilian populations into committing acts of violence against other civilians and state forces.

Almost a century ago, the international community dealt with fascism. Less than a half-century ago, communism was perceived to be a blister on society. The formation, collapse, and reconstruction of states and the Eastern bloc were related to changes in the way wars were fought and in where and how they were fought. Although terrorism is not a new phenomenon, the recent decades have been marked by an increase in religiously ideological terrorism and Islamist-jihadists manipulating supportive civilian populations into committing acts of violence against other civilians and state forces.

For decision makers and people, who confront it, Islamic terrorism creates dilemmas due to its rapid and shape-shifting advances. By exploiting liberal values, it challenges the use of effective and balanced counterterrorism policies for the Western world and liberal democratic states in general.

This chapter aims to provide an overview of terrorism. Section 2.1 begins with a debate on a useful definition of terrorism because the understanding and agreement on what qualifies an attack as an act of terrorism and simultaneously distinguishes it from other forms and phenomena, will have extensive implications for both theoretical and practical considerations. A consensus is essential to any serious attempt to combat terrorism (Zeidan 2006, p. 217).

Subsequently, the causes of terrorism and the motivations of men to engage in terrorist activities are tackled in Sect. 2.2 as they provide a starting point to not only explain but also to fight terrorism.

© The Author(s), under exclusive license to Springer Nature Switzerland AG 2020

N. Ismael, *Strategic Interaction Between Islamist Terror Groups*, SpringerBriefs in Economics, https://doi.org/10.1007/978-3-030-51307-8_2

Section 2.3, then, explores the economic impacts of terrorism. By considering the effects of terrorist incidents on households, the private sector, and the government, the chapter tries to address the economic dimensions of terrorism.

2.1 In Search of a Definition

The use of the term terrorism can be traced back to the French Revolution's Reign of Terror. In order to compel obedience to the state and to intimidate regime enemies, the Jacobins, who ruled the revolutionary state, employed, for example, mass executions by guillotine. Early uses were almost exclusively made in the context of the state, and its association with state violence and intimidation lasted until the mid-nineteenth century, when it began to be associated with nongovernmental groups (Tilly 2004, pp. 5–6).

Although definitions of terrorism nowadays are often just small variations of each other, the debate on how to define terrorism and the attempt to find an agreement continue. This is partly based upon the fear that one's practices or those of one's allies will be condemned as terrorism. Edward Peck, former Deputy Director of the White House Task Force on Terrorism under Ronald Reagan, stated that "*in 1985, [. . .] we produced about six [definitions], and each and every case, they were rejected, because carefully reading would indicate that our own country had been involved in some of these activities.*"[1]

One option for approaching the issue is to point to the (more or less) accepted international laws and principles set out by the Hague and the Geneva Conventions. These laws regulate, which behaviors are allowed or forbidden during wartime and are premised on the intentional harming of soldiers in conventional wars as an admitted imperative, whereas the deliberate targeting of civilians is prohibited. It is widely accepted that terrorism erodes these rules of war, raising issues concerning state terrorism since almost every government in the world has violated these rules of war. Some emphasize the legitimization of a state by its monopoly of power, so that a state terrorism is logically impossible because of the very definition[2] of a state (Primoratz 2005, p. 72; Laqueur 2003, p. 237). An additional argument was made by the former Secretary-General of the United Nations, Kofi Annan, who remarked that the use of force by states is already regulated under international law, and any governing body's abusive behavior is addressed according to the established rules and regulations (Report of the Secretary-General 2005, p. 26).

The United Nations' approach is problematic because it rests upon the belief that violent acts of states are indeed addressed in their entirety and accepted by all. Furthermore, it does not tackle the question on how to handle successful terrorist

---

[1]Passage from an interview with Amy Goodman, Democracy Now, July 28, 2006.

[2]Stalin's USSR, Nazi Germany, and probably Assad's Syria, however, contradict such a position.

groups that may build up a state, or a state-like authority, as had been temporarily the case for *Daesh* in Syria.

Similar issues arise when addressing what constitutes a terrorist and what does not. The answer is very much guided by the subjective perspective of the definer and hinges on whether a person sides with the attackers or their victims because "*one man's terrorist is another man's freedom fighter*" (Jenkins 1982, p. 12).

At the core of most definitions is the use of violence or the threat of violence intended to achieve a political goal, implying that terror groups are primarily politically motivated. Although ultimate goals and desires change over time, Kydd and Walter (2006, p. 52) identify five essential objectives: status quo maintenance, social control, regime change, policy change, and territorial change, all of which contribute to a political agenda. Some terrorist movements aim at multiple goals which, in turn, depend on each other.

The focus on solely political objectives is not useful, when considering terrorist attacks that are caused by religious or other ideological motivations. Notably, Islamic-jihadist-based terrorism, which intends to secure and protect sacred lands as well as to expand a particular culture, has become increasingly relevant today (Acharya 2008, p. 654). The ultimate desire of *al-Qaeda* and *Daesh*, for example, is to establish global jihadism. Their motivation is, thus, distinctly religious in tone. Nevertheless, religious purposes may translate into political ends.

Despite varying refinements, political scientists, economists, and political economists are converging on a consensus based on an operational definition and have agreed upon the main aspects of terrorism, namely the perpetrators, the victims, and the resonant mass. Such harmony is crucial as it provides a base for theoretical considerations, including game theory, and datasets to test theoretical propositions.

The perpetrators are non-state actors, i.e., subnational groups, associated individuals, copy-cats, or lone wolfs. The resonant mass refers to the collective terror groups want to intimidate (Thornton 1964, pp. 78–79). However, each terror group has several target audiences to which it strives to communicate different messages (Ganor 2005, p. 235). While a definition of terrorism implicitly involves the downside of terrorist behavior, the demoralizing nature, terror groups also send their messages to a potential followership.

Terrorism then is the premeditated use or threat to use violence by subnational groups or individuals to obtain a political or social objective through the intimidation of a large audience beyond that of the immediate victims (Enders and Sandler 2012, p. 4).

Although this working definition[3] avoids specifying the victims, many scientists stress the intentionally targeting of civilians by terrorists to draw a definitory line to other modes of violence. In this light, attacks against regular armies are not viewed

---

[3]This description is very much in line with the definition of the US Department of Defense (DoD), which describes terrorism as "*the unlawful use of violence or threat of violence to instill fear and coerce governments or societies. Terrorism is often motivated by religious, political, or other ideological beliefs and committed in pursuit of goals that are usually political*" (Department of Defense 2014, p. vii).

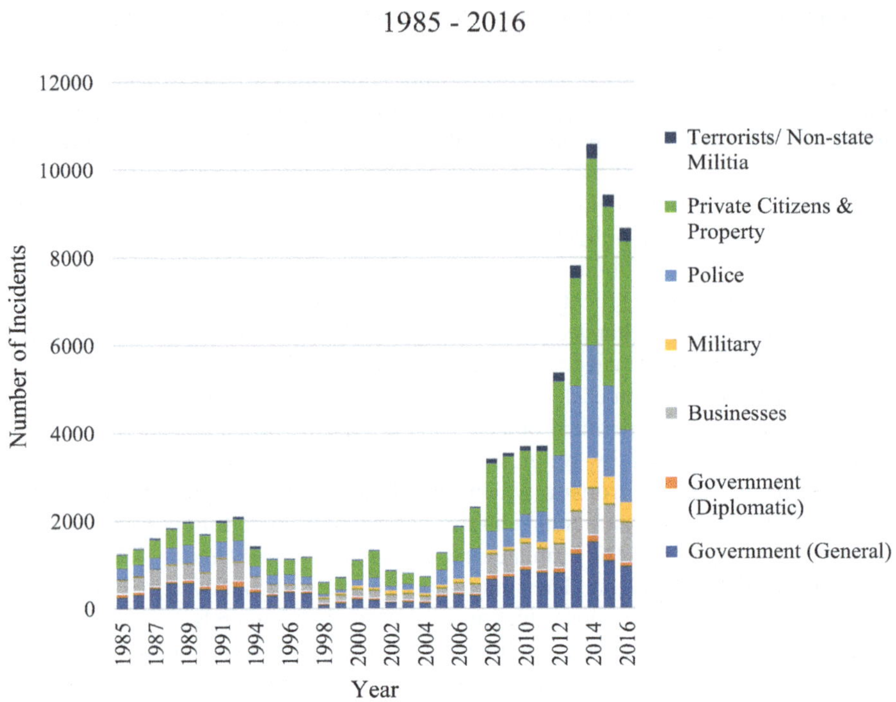

Fig. 2.1 Number of incidents and target types, 1985–2016. Source: Global Terrorist Database. Note: Overall, the GTD incorporates 22 target types. For this thesis, only the seven most interesting target types were selected

as terrorism, even though they occupy lands as the US forces did in Afghanistan or Iraq, whereas an attack against peacekeepers is considered to be a terrorist incident.

As shown in Fig. 2.1, in most cases private citizens and property have been targeted by terrorist groups as well as government targets.

Proportionally, military targets have become more and more popular since the beginning of the twenty-first century. Notwithstanding, military targets remain less important and do only account for a small proportion of terror incidents. Hence, the debate concerning whether a useful definition of terrorism must include only non-combatants is pointless, partly merely because the number of attacks against military targets is proportionally small.

2.2 What Makes a Terrorist?

The questions on why terrorism is more likely in some settings than in others and why some individuals are willing to give up their lives to cause damage, always revolve around the attempt to find a typical pattern of causation. Identifying the causes and finding a general explanation for the emergence of terrorism, would ostensibly provide a solid starting point for countermeasures.

The structure of terrorist groups can differ, some are organized as networks, and others act unilaterally. In general, the supportive audience of terrorist groups is modeled as a pyramid of support[4] with its leadership at the peak of a much broader movement dedicated to the same ideology or political agenda. The leadership is deeply committed and usually includes charismatic figures. It defines policy and directs actions, while the cadre comprises the most active members, who carry out the attacks and are also extremely committed. In contrast to the cadre, active supporters do not carry out attacks but assist the group with, among others, money, information, or safe houses. Passive supporters are sympathetic to the terrorists' cause but cannot or will not assist the group directly (McCauley and Moskalenko 2008, p. 418).

Even though motivations to establish or to participate in a terrorist organization may vary, the literature on terrorism identifies two theoretical explanations, economic deprivation as well as political and institutional issues respectively. Both economic and political factors are assumed to increase grievances, which take shape in the presence of a gap between desired payoffs and actual payoffs of individuals, and to lower the opportunity costs for violence (Gurr 1970, p. 45).

Poor structural economic conditions create frustration that makes violence and, thus, terrorism more likely. Weak economic conditions such as inequality, unemployment, or less education were positively associated with the genesis of terrorism (Collier and Hoeffler 2004). In environments where relative economic deprivation dominates, terrorist organizations should find it easier, i.e., less costly, to recruit followers or to receive funding from supporters (Robison et al. 2006, p. 2011). Not least, former US president George W. Bush (CNN 2002) stated that "*we fight against poverty because hope is an answer to terror*," thus, linking terrorism and poverty, and indicating that a fight against poverty breeds terrorism. The alleged connection between poverty, lack of education, and terrorism caused efforts to improve economic and educational opportunities. However, only a few case studies[5] provide empirical support. Other studies do not find a significant relationship between economic conditions and the emergence of terrorism, particularly when not addressing country-specific cases, but cross-country patterns. Krueger and Laitin (2008), Krueger and Maleckova (2003), and Piazza (2006), for instance, do not find any evidence that poverty generates terrorism. Also, the 9/11 Commission Report emphasized: "*Terrorism is not caused by poverty*" (National Commission on Terrorist Attacks upon the United States 2004, p. 378).

Also, Testas (2004), who focuses on several Muslim countries, shows that per capita income is not strongly connected to terrorism but is instead strongly

[4]An alternative is the so-called onion model, in which an organization is imbedded within an aggrieved population in a series of successively larger rings (Pruitt 2006, p. 375).

[5]See, for example, Samaranayake (1999), Testas (2001), Saleh (2004, 2009), and Cotte (2011) for case-studies.

connected to political factors. The findings are supported by Piazza (2007), who notes that determinants such as political stability surpass economic ones for the Middle East region.

Instead of being drawn from the ranks of the poor and poorly educated, survey data show that terrorists from different movements are predominantly recruited from relatively wealthy and educated family backgrounds (Krueger and Maleckova 2003; Testas 2004; Berrebi 2007; Azam and Thelen 2008). Krueger and Maleckova (2003) argue that this is a consequence of an increased interest in politics that is associated with better education and a more privileged background. Also, better education of potential terrorists makes it more likely for them to be successful, making them more attractive recruits for terrorist activity (Bueno de Mesquita 2005, p. 256). This positive association is also explicitly found for suicide bombers (Benmelech and Berrebi 2007).

The mixed empirical results on the relation of terrorism and economic deprivation suggest that economic determinants do only play a minor role in the decision to participate in terrorism. Political instability and repression appear to be more important to the decision to engage in terrorism instead. State failure, for example, is supposed to be a significant driver in the emergence of terrorist groups as it, ostensibly, provides a low-cost environment and, in some cases, safe havens (Rotberg 2002). The weakness of states due to state frailty or changes in the political system creates a political vacuum, which allows terrorists to push their agendas, because an unstable government may be too weak to challenge terrorism and, thus, makes it less costly. Additionally, if there are few non-violent alternatives, individuals may be attracted by radical organizations (Campos and Gassebner 2009). The rise of jihadism across the Middle East and North Africa due to state failures may serve as an example. Many states in these regions are now weaker than they were ten years ago. Four have either collapsed or have come close. Others' long-term sustainability is in doubt. The challenges are over the states' abilities to deliver basic services. The instability has allowed extremist movements to embed themselves politically and then exploit them physically. The correlation is evident in the 2016 Fragile State Index: the four countries that have deteriorated the most over the previous decade are Libya, Syria, Mali, and Yemen. Terrorist groups such as *al-Qaeda* and *Daesh* have exploited the failure of traditional states to advance their agendas (Fund for Peace 2016).

These developments are reinforced by civilizational clashes, when groups exhibit different identities in the sense of different ethnicities, religion, or interpretations of a particular religion (Huntington 1996). When terrorist organizations build on identity-related ideologies that stress their supremacy or the inferiority of other identities, it should be easier to gather support (Basuchoudhary and Shughart 2010). The Middle East region, for example, experienced an ideological upheaval. Extremist organizations have presented themselves as the defenders of the Sunni population against Alawites, Shiites, Christians, and Jews. The combination of states' frailty and a retreat to more basic forms of identity eliminates moral constraints and strengthens an organization's coherence (Bernholz 2006).

Apart from a political vacuum, in which terrorists can thrive, repression has been perceived to cause terrorism. Increased repression may signal to terrorist groups and their sympathizers that protest and violence are not only justified but also worthy (Frey and Luechinger 2002). Foreign intervention may work in a similar manner (Addison and Mansoob Murshed 2005). As will be shown in Chap. 6, several of the most turning points in the rise of jihadi groups have involved foreign intervention.

While the formation of terror groups usually is induced by a superior aim and a certain path dependency, individuals that decide to participate may be inspired by the group's purpose. However, some may have more mundane reasons. In any case, terror organizations rely on recruitment to push their agendas and to conduct attacks. While virtually everyone can conduct small and simple incidents, more complex and spectacular attacks call for more capable members.

2.3 The Economic Impacts of Terrorism

> We are continuing this policy in bleeding America to the point of bankruptcy. Allah willing, and nothing is too great for Allah.[6]

Even if Osama bin Laden did not mean economic bankruptcy, terrorism can have serious economic impacts. When considering the unprecedented magnitude of 9/11, direct and indirect economic losses have become essential points of discussion within the terrorism literature. The physical destruction of buildings and infrastructure as well as human losses, which amounted to over 3000, far exceeded the average scale of a terrorist attack. Although the 9/11 incidents present an outlier, most emphasis has been put on evaluating the effects arising from the aftermath of this unprecedented event. Estimates concerning the direct human and capital costs of 9/11 range between US$ 25 and US$ 60 billion (Navarro and Spencer 2001).

The immediate costs can be determined concerning the economic value of the property destroyed and the lives lost and are usually derived by estimating the present market value of the projected future production of the lost physical and human assets. This does not imply that all losses associated with terrorism can be reduced to purely market calculations. The psychological costs, e.g., suffering and fear, of terrorism on victims and their families as well as on other survivors are quite real, but the methods of quantifying these costs are usually insufficient. Moreover, the economic impact of terrorist attacks is not limited to the apparent losses; it also includes losses in production, e.g., profits and rents as well as income from wages, from the destroyed assets. Further, it contains potential disruptions in national and international markets, changes in consumer and investor confidence, increased costs of risk, and other social impacts which may translate into economic losses.

[6] Osama bin Laden transcript released by Al-Jazeera November 2004.

Estimating these impacts requires considering not only the direct physical losses and casualties but also for the indirect effects that emerge because of the distortion of the economy and actions to alleviate the damages.

In general, terrorist incidents affect three types of sectors: households, the private sector and producers, respectively, and the public sector, represented by the government. These agents are affected differently, and all are considered in more detail.

2.3.1 Effects on Households

Terrorist incidents are associated with harm and uncertainty, which impact upon individual utility beyond the direct losses. These psychological, nonmonetary impacts can directly translate into monetary factors, when, for example, they change consumption behavior or negatively impact labor productivity (Naor 2006).

Changes in consumption have been particularly considered. Eckstein and Tsiddon (2004) illustrate that terrorism reduces economic activity. They find a considerable reduction in the consumption of nondurables due to terrorism in Israel which they associate with a change in utility resulting from increased terrorist activity (Eckstein and Tsiddon 2004, p. 993). These findings are confirmed by Llussá and Tavares (2011), who show that private consumption is negatively affected by terrorism, by collating data from 168 countries.

A more interesting result is presented by Enders and Sandler (2005). Contrary to intuition, the direct response to 9/11 had been an increase in consumption of durable goods. They explain that the rise in demand in the immediate aftermath of the 9/11 attacks is associated with an increased patriotic consciousness and setting in defiance (Enders and Sandler 2005, pp. 296–297). In contrast to Enders and Sandler, who relate increased consumption to the past attacks on the World Trade Center and the Pentagon, Shieh et al. (2005) believe that the expectation concerning future attacks, which were announced by *al-Qaeda* and found to be credible by the government, explains the increase in consumer demand. When households are fully informed and expect terrorist attacks shortly, they may be incentivized to increase their consumption of durable goods as a reaction to a potentially shortened lifespan (Shieh et al. 2005, p. 415).

In order to account for nonmonetary effects, some approaches link a loss in life satisfaction and welfare to fear and insecurity resulting from terrorist attacks. Although fear is highly subjective, economic methods such as the hedonic evaluation approach or the contingent valuation method can be employed to estimate the "price" of fear. Life satisfaction or happiness, then, is a proxy measure of an individual's utility. Frey and Luechinger (2005) and Frey et al. (2009) combine indicators of welfare with terror indicators to analyze the impacts of terrorism on life satisfaction in France, the Republic of Ireland, and the United Kingdom. For all three countries, the estimates show that terrorist attacks have a statistically significant negative effect on reported life satisfaction, implying massive utility losses. This decrease in well-being is, among other things, reflected in the hypothetical willingness of people to pay for a reduction of terrorism. Individuals would need to receive substantial increases in income to compensate for the harm inflicted by terrorism (Frey et al. 2009, p. 340).

Although the sources of fear are a psychological rather than an economic problem,[7] even the economic literature strives for explanations of some determinants of anxiety caused by terrorism. In this regard, Becker and Rubinstein (2011) note that exogenous shocks in general, and terrorist attacks in particular, influence individuals through two mechanisms: changes to hazard potential and changes in anxiety (Becker and Rubinstein 2011, p. 7), both resulting in a decrease of utility.

One factor discussed is the phenomenon of "*probability-neglect*" (Sunstein 2003). Sunstein (2003) shows that individuals tend to focus on the badness of an event's outcome rather than on the probability that it will happen. Such an "irrational" evaluation of risk on the part of individuals is induced by an outcome-independent variable of "fear and loathing" that greatly exceeds the objective, i.e., true, discounted harm. The degree to which subjective beliefs about hazards deviate from objective assessments of risk may then explain people's "irrational" responses to terrorism (Kahneman and Tversky 1973). Furthermore, people base their risk analysis on cognitive experiences of past events rather than on actual probabilities of future events. That is, they employ the "*availability heuristic*" (Kunreuther 2002, P. 658), leading to an overestimation of a terrorist attack, which is usually characterized as a low-probability event causing a high impact. In contrast, certain events that are more likely but cause a smaller effect, e.g., car accidents, maybe systematically underestimated (Sandler and Enders 2004). This notion is supported by Gigerenzer (2006), who finds that Americans cut back air travel after 9/11 to avoid being killed in the course of a low-probability attack. In other words, terrorist incidents, although less likely to happen to the ordinary citizen, will produce more fear than more probable risks (Downes-Le Guin and Hoffman 1993).

The distorted perception of terrorist attacks provides terror organizations with an advantage. While ignoring daily risks and overestimating unlikely catastrophic events, terrorist groups produce society-wide fear. Although these anomalies also occur in other contexts, Viscusi and Zeckhauser (2003) show that they are especially relevant in the case of terrorism. They find that people tend to assume worst-case scenarios in assessing terrorism risks and are prone to anomalies (Viscusi and Zeckhauser 2003, pp. 113–114).

2.3.2 *Effects on the Private Sector*

In October 2000, a motorboat equipped with explosive materials rammed the *USS Cole* in Yemen. Two years later, Yemeni terrorists attacked the French tanker *Limburg* while it was readying to receive its cargo of crude oil from an offshore

[7]For psychological impacts see, for example, Sacco et al. (2003).

terminal. Although Yemen is ideally located as a major Middle Eastern port, because it borders the Red Sea and the Arabian Sea, the combined attacks on the *Limburg* and the *USS Cole* ruined Yemen's shipping industry. According to a US Department of State fact sheet, these two incidents sufficed to induce the Yemeni government to expect a loss of US$ 3.8 million per month as a result of a 50% decrease in port activity (U.S. Department of State fact sheet 2002).

Companies have been directly and indirectly affected by terrorism for a long time. As Fig. 2.1 illustrated, businesses globally have become more and more targeted since 2006. Firms not only source from and supply to, but also operate in troubled countries, thus exposing themselves to greater threats of terrorism. Further, substitution effects of terrorists who shift their attention from better-protected targets toward relatively easier targets[8] may result in an increase of attacks against businesses.

The direct losses of terrorist attacks depend on the characteristics of the attacked companies but also on the nature of an attack and its impacts, which may include property damage and ransom payments for hostages.

Even if businesses do not directly experience physical destruction, terrorism can affect firms by increasing their overall level of market and credit risk (invalid source). Furthermore, the danger of business interruptions has received much attention in the literature. It has been estimated that supply chain interruptions accounted for one-third of the entire losses from 9/11 (Kleindorfer and Saad 2005).

It is not the shock per se that create cataclysmic events, but vulnerabilities of the economic system, which determine the impacts of an exogenous shock, such as a terrorist attack. This is important insofar as reducing the economic effects of terrorism should, then, not only focus on the actual threat but also on the extent to which the economic system has become more resilient or more vulnerable (Kunreuther 2006).

The threat of terrorism may make a country more vulnerable and increase public demand for security. Such increases in security may negatively affect economic efficiency, for example, by producing overhead investment in public security and emergency response (Kunreuther 2006).

Some industries and sectors will be more affected by terrorism than others. Tourism, travel, and entertainment events will probably experience a reduced demand, or there will be a change in the composition of demand away from activities that are perceived to be likely terrorist targets toward others that are not.

The insurance industry will also be affected. Not only will more claims be the result of terrorist attacks but an increase in terrorism or the perceived threat of terrorism will increase actual risk and, in turn, will increase the demand for insurance. An increase in the costs of insurance, and, in relation to this, security, will increase production costs. As a result, firms will experience a leftward shift in their supply curves, mainly where security represents an essential part of their costs. It is

[8]A detailed explanation of the substitution effect on part of terrorists is given in Chap. 4.

also possible that increased stockpiling of some primary products and raw materials will drive up their price shifting supply curves further to the left (Bird et al. 2008).

The insurance sector plays a somewhat unique role as it does not experience destruction directly but suffers under the consequences of terrorism through ensuing payment claims. While insurance companies can cover small terror attacks, 9/11 dealt a blow to the insurance sector—firstly, due to claims at the scale of billions of dollars and, secondly, due to negative impacts on stock markets.

The main problem was the number and volume of simultaneous claims, exceeding the total capital held by insurance companies. Claims on insurance related to 9/11 totaled US$ 50 to US$ 80 billion (Alexander and Alexander 2002). As a consequence, the insurance sector reacted by raising premiums dramatically (between 50 and 100%), which hit the shipping and transportation companies[9] and owners of large commercial properties particularly hard (Walkenhorst and Dihel 2002). Moreover, 9/11 and the unquantifiable risk associated with terror events induced insurance companies to exclude the coverage of terrorism unless government support was granted. The intervention of the government in the insurance market, which under normal conditions counters liberal market philosophies, may present an instance where public intervention and even subsidies are necessary for maintaining some market forces rather than using regulation to stifle the market for terror insurance (Brown et al. 2004).

Another important sector is the tourism industry. Tourists were frequently targeted by terrorists in recent years.[10] Attacks on tourist and tourist spots generate huge media attention and cause revenue losses as tourists redirect their vacation plans to relatively safer areas (Frey et al. 2007). Enders and Sandler (1991) applied a VAR methodology to Spain for the 1970–1991 period, during which time ETA and other groups waged terrorist campaigns. Each transnational terrorist incident was estimated to dissuade over 140,000 tourists, a number that can translate into a sizable amount of lost revenue. Enders et al. (1992) also found that terrorism had a significant negative, lagged influence on tourism. Terrorism is particularly detrimental to countries for which tourism is an important source of revenue.

Just as tourists avoid areas likely to suffer a terrorist attack, international investors are likely to avoid high-terrorism areas. Obviously, a terrorist attack can destroy infrastructure and cause business disruptions. Firms also seek to avoid the increased costs necessary to protect facilities from potential attacks. Such costs include those of directly securing facilities, maintaining security clearances for employees, and additional insurance charges. Terrorist threats increase the costs of doing business, as expensive security measures must be deployed, and personnel must be compensated, both of which reduce the returns to net foreign direct investments (NFDI). As

[9]Airlines faced an increase of insurance premiums of up to 400%; yet, this was buffered thanks to the airline stability legislation, which allows for the federal government to pay any rise in commercial insurance (Alexander and Alexander 2002).

[10]It is argued that higher security measures for military and governmental facilities made tourists relatively more attractive for terrorist attacks (Im et al. 1987).

terrorist risks rise, investors will redirect their investments to safer areas and countries, so that foreign firms will seek safer locations for their facilities and domestic firms will seek to locate abroad (Enders and Sandler 1996).

Chen and Siems (2004), who studied the impacts of terrorist events on the US capital market in comparison to other military attacks such as the invasion of North Korea in 1950 or the invasion of Kuwait, 1990, illustrated that military attacks led to substantial negative cumulative returns. In contrast, the event of terrorist bombing attacks (Pan Am, 1988; World Trade Center, 1993; Oklahoma, 1995; or the US embassy in Kenya 1998) did not produce abnormal returns. The only exception was 9/11: the attacks significantly impacted markets that showed negative cumulative abnormal returns even after six trading days. Nevertheless, Chen and Siems conclude that the magnitude of the shock was less severe than responses to previous shocks (2004, p. 360). In agreement with others (Sandler and Enders 2008; Brück 2007), they argued that the contained shocks of financial and stock markets are primarily due to increased resilience of US capital markets to exogenous shocks.

More developed—and thus more resilient—markets are expected to react less to singular terrorist attacks, even in the scale of 9/11. Arin et al. (2008) confirm the idea that the magnitude of the effects depends on the level of development of the attacked markets. Compared to large-scale singular events, protracted attacks in smaller markets can have significant impacts. Eldor and Melnick (2004), who analyzed the impacts of protracted terrorist attacks on stock and foreign exchange markets in Israel, found that suicide bombings have permanent effects on both markets; overall, the Israeli–Palestinian conflict reduced the stock market capitalization substantially (Elder and Melnick, 2004, p. 383). Zussman and Zussman (2006) also find that the Israeli stock markets react to news linked to terrorism and counterterrorism. In Zussman et al. (2008), periods of violence are associated with a decrease in asset prices, while periods of peace increase asset prices. This finding is in line with the previously reported ones and indicates that markets react to terrorist violence in predictable ways.

Overall, Sandler and Enders (2008) conclude that markets and sectors are likely to recover quickly from terrorist attacks even if some may face significant losses, given that the economy is not confronted with sustained terrorist incidents. While the direct physical damage without a doubt hurt companies, 9/11 has shown that it is disruptions in the interconnected economy, which impact businesses more severely. The effects of a large-scale singular attack in a comparatively well-diversified capital and stock market may be relatively short-lived and small, the impact of protracted terror events, even if small in scale and in relatively less diversified markets, may create lasting negative impacts.

2.3.3 Effects on Governments

Various studies estimated the costs resulting from 9/11. Navarro and Spencer (2001), for example, computed that human capital losses alone amount to US$ 40 billion.

The destruction of property was estimated to amount to US$ 14 to the private sector, US$ 1.5 billion for state and local government enterprises, and US$ 0.7 billion for the US federal government. Rescue and clean-up costs had been estimated to sum up to US$ 11 billion, where the latter was shared between the private and the public sector (Lenain et al. 2002, p. 6).

While these numbers stress the direct consequences of 9/11, a policy response in the aftermath of terrorist attacks does not only contain crisis management taken by the authority to mitigate the economic impacts but also appropriate emergency response preparedness before an attack. Particularly large-scale attacks, just like natural disasters, will pose a major challenge for the public health infrastructure. It has not only to deal with mass casualties in the direct aftermath of an attack but will also have long-term effects concerning physical and psychological consequences (Hyams et al. 2002). Fiscal policies responding to the impacts of spectacular events include the implementation of tax cuts and tax stimulus packages. Only a few days after 9/11 the US Congress approved an emergency spending package of US$ 40 billion for reconstruction and increased security measures. Furthermore, the government granted support to the amount of US$ 15 billion to the aviation industry (Baily 2001, p. 3).

Generally, long-term impacts on governments are difficult to assess. This is particularly true for the rise in national defense and domestic security spending, which may divert resources away from other public spending areas. Whereas small-scale attacks can be assumed to have little effect on national budgets as they usually do not entail the consequences 9/11 had, large-scale attacks will inevitably raise budgets.

References

Acharya UD (2008) War on terror or terror wars: the problem in defining terrorism. Denv J Int'l L Pol'y 37(4):653–679

Addison T, Mansoob Murshed S (2005) Transnational terrorism as a spillover of domestic disputes in other countries. Defence Peace Econ 16(2):69–82

Alexander DC, Alexander Y (2002) Terrorism and business: the impact of September 11, 2001. Brill | Nijhoff, Leiden

Arin KP, Ciferri D, Spagnolo N (2008) The price of terror: the effects of terrorism on stock market returns and volatility. Econ Lett 101(3):164–167

Azam J-P, Thelen V (2008) The roles of foreign aid and education in the war on terror. Public Choice 135(3–4):375–397

Baily MN (2001) Economic policy following the terrorist attacks. Policy Briefs PB01–10, Peterson Institute for International Economics

Basuchoudhary A, Shughart WF (2010) On ethnic conflict and the origins of transnational terrorism. Defence Peace Econ 21(1):65–87

Becker GS, Rubinstein Y (2011) Fear and the response to terrorism: an economic analysis. University of Chicago. CEP Discussion Paper No.1079

Benmelech E, Berrebi C (2007) Human capital and the productivity of suicide bombers. J Econ Perspect 21(3):223–238

Bernholz P (2006) International political system, supreme values and terrorism. Public Choice 128 (1–2):221–231
Berrebi C (2007) Evidence about the link between education, poverty and terrorism among Palestinians. Peace Econ Peace Sci Public Policy 13(1):1–36
Bird G, Brock Blomberg S, Hess GD (2008) International terrorism: causes, consequences and cures. World Econ 31(2):255–274
Brown JR, David Cummins J, Lewis CM, Wei R (2004) An empirical analysis of the economic impact of federal terrorism reinsurance. J Monet Econ 51(5):861–898
Brück T (2007) The economic analysis of terrorism. Routledge, Abingdon
Bueno de Mesquita E (2005) The quality of terror. Am J Polit Sci 49(3):515–530
Campos NF, Gassebner M (2009) International terrorism, political instability and the escalation effect. IZA Discussion Paper No. 4061
Chen AH, Siems TF (2004) The effects of terrorism on global capital markets. Eur J Polit Econ 20 (2):349–366
CNN (2002) Bush ties poverty aid boost to social reform. Accessed 23 Aug 2018. http://edition.cnn.com/2002/WORLD/americas/03/22/bush.latin/index.html?related
Collier P, Hoeffler A (2004) Greed and grievance in civil war. Oxf Econ Pap 56(4):563–595
Cotte Poveda A (2011) Socio-economic development and violence: an empirical application for seven metropolitan areas in Colombia. Peace Econ Peace Sci Public Policy 17(1):1–23
Downes-Le Guin T, Hoffman B (1993) The impact of terrorism on public opinion. RAND Corporation
Eckstein Z, Tsiddon D (2004) Macroeconomic consequences of terror: theory and the case of Israel. J Monet Econ 51(5):971–1002
Eldor R, Melnick R (2004) Financial markets and terrorism. Eur J Polit Econ 20(2):367–386
Enders W, Sandler T (1991) Causality between transnational terrorism and tourism: the case of Spain. Stud Confl Terror 14(1):49–58
Enders W, Sandler T (1996) Terrorism and foreign direct investment in Spain and Greece. Kyklos 49(3):331–352
Enders W, Sandler T (2005) After 9/11: is it all different now? J Confl Resolut 49(2):259–277
Enders W, Sandler T (2012) The political economy of terrorism, 2nd edn. Cambridge University Press, Cambridge
Enders W, Sandler T, Parise GF (1992) An econometric analysis of the impact of terrorism on tourism. Kyklos 45(4):531–554
Frey BS, Luechinger S (2002) Terrorism: deterrence may backfire. Zurich IEER Working Paper No. 136
Frey BS, Luechinger S (2005) Measuring terrorism. In: Marciano A, Josselin J-M (eds) Law and the state: a political economy approach. Edward Elgar Publishing, Cheltenham, pp 142–182
Frey BS, Luechinger S, Stutzer A (2007) Calculating tragedy: assessing the costs of terrorism. J Econ Surv 21(1):1–24
Frey BS, Luechinger S, Stutzer A (2009) The life satisfaction approach to valuing public goods: the case of terrorism. Public Choice 138(3–4):317–345
Fund for Peace (2016) Fragile state index 2016. In: Messner JJ (ed) Fund for Peace, Washington, DC. Accessed 21 May 2018. http://fundforpeace.org/fsi/wp-content/uploads/2017/05/Fragile-States-Index-Annual-Report-2016-ver-3e.pdf
Ganor B (2005) The counter-terrorism puzzle: a guide for decision makers. Transaction Publisher, New Brunswick, NJ
Gigerenzer G (2006) Out of the frying pan into the fire: behavioral reactions to terrorist attacks. Risk Anal 26(2):347–351
Gurr TR (1970) Why men rebel. Princeton University Press, Princeton
Huntington SP (1996) The clash of civilizations and the remaking of world order. Simon & Schuster, New York

Hyams KC, Murphy FM, Wessely S (2002) Responding to chemical, biological, or nuclear terrorism: the indirect and long-term health effects may present the greatest challenge. J Health Polit Policy Law 27(2):273–292

Im EI, Cauley J, Sandler T (1987) Cycles and substitutions in terrorist activities: a spectral approach. Kyklos 40(2):238–255

Jenkins BM (1982) Statements about terrorism. Ann Am Acad Pol Soc Sci 463(1):11–23

Kahneman D, Tversky A (1973) On the psychology of prediction. Psychol Rev 80(4):237–251

Kleindorfer PR, Saad GH (2005) Managing disruption risks in supply chains. Prod Oper Manag 14 (1):53–68

Krueger AB, Laitin DD (2008) Kto Kogo?: A cross-country study of the origins and targets of terrorism. In: Keefer P, Loayza N (eds) Terrorism, economic development, and political openness. Cambridge University Press, Cambridge, pp 148–173

Krueger AB, Maleckova J (2003) Education, poverty and terrorism: is there a causal connection? J Econ Perspect 17(4):119–144

Kunreuther H (2002) Risk analysis and risk management in an uncertain world. Risk Anal 22 (4):655–664

Kunreuther H (2006) Risk and reaction. Harv Int Rev 28(3):37–42

Kydd AH, Walter BF (2006) The strategies of terrorism. Int Secur 31(1):49–80

Laqueur W (2003) No end to war: terrorism in the twenty-first century. Continuum International Publishing Group

Lenain P, Bonturi M, Koen V (2002) The economic consequences of terrorism. OECD Economics Department Working Papers No. 334

Llussá F, Tavares J (2011) Which terror at which cost? On the economic consequences of terrorist attacks. Econ Lett 110(1):52–55

McCauley C, Moskalenko S (2008) Mechanisms of political radicalization: pathways toward terrorism. Terror Polit Violence 20(3):415–433

Naor Z (2006) Untimely death, the value of certain lifetime and macroeconomic dynamics. Defence Peace Econ 17(4):343–359

National Commission on Terrorist Attacks upon the United States (2004) The 9/11 commission report. Accessed 14 Aug 2018. http://govinfo.library.unt.edu/911/report/911Report.pdf

Navarro P, Spencer A (2001) September 11, 2001: assessing the costs of terrorism. Milken Inst Rev 2:16–31

Piazza JA (2006) Rooted in poverty?: Terrorism, poor economic development, and social cleavages. Terror Polit Violence 18(1):159–177

Piazza JA (2007) Draining the swamp: democracy promotion, state failure, and terrorism in 19 Middle Eastern countries. Stud Confl Terror 30(6):521–539

Primoratz I (2005) State terrorism and counter-terrorism. In: Meggle G (ed) Ethics of terrorism and counter-terrorism, vol 3. Ontos Verlag, Frankfurt, pp 69–81

Pruitt D (2006) Negotiation with terrorists. Int Negot 11(2):371–394

Report of the Secretary-General (2005) In larger freedom: towards development, security and human rights for all. *United Nations*, A/59/2005. Accessed 3 Oct 2018. http://undocs.org/A/59/2005

Robison KK, Crenshaw EM, Craig Jenkins J (2006) Ideologies of violence: the social origins of Islamist and leftist transnational terrorism. Soc Forces 84(4):2009–2026

Rotberg RI (2002) The new nature of nation-state failure. Wash Q 25(3):83–96

Sacco K, Galletto V, Blanzieri E (2003) How has the 9/11 terrorist attack influenced decision making? Appl Cognit Psychol 17(9):1113–1127

Saleh BA (2004) Economic conditions and resistance to occupation in the West Bank and Gaza Strip: there is a causal connection. Top Middle East North Afr Econ 6:1–27

Saleh B (2009) An econometric analysis of Palestinian attacks: an examination of deprivation theory and choice of attacks. Eur J Soc Sci 7(4):17–29

Samaranayake G (1999) Patterns of political violence and responses of the government in Sri Lanka 1971–1996. Terror Polit Violence 11(1):110–122

Sandler T, Enders W (2004) An economic perspective on transnational terrorism. Eur J Polit Econ 20(2):301–316

Sandler T, Enders W (2008) Economic consequences of terrorism in developed and developing countries. In: Keefer P, Loayza N (eds) Terrorism, economic development, and political openness. Cambridge University Press, Cambridge, pp 17–47

Shieh J-Y, Chen J-H, Chang J-J, Lai C-C (2005) Terrorist threats and transitional dynamics in an overlapping generations model. Defence Peace Econ 16(6):415–425

Sunstein CR (2003) Terrorism and probability neglect. J Risk Uncertain 26(2–3):121–136

Testas A (2001) The economic causes of Algeria's political violence. Terror Polit Violence 13 (3):127–144

Testas A (2004) Determinants of terrorism in the Muslim world: an empirical cross-sectional analysis. Terror Polit Violence 16(2):253–273

Thornton TP (1964) Terror as a weapon of political agitation. In: Eckstein H (ed) Internal war: problems and approaches. Free Press, New York, pp 71–99

Tilly C (2004) Terror, terrorism, terrorists. Sociol Theory 22(1):5–13

United States Department of Defense (2014) Counterterrorism. Joint Publication 3–26. Accessed 3 Sept 2018. https://www.jcs.mil/Portals/36/Documents/Doctrine/pubs/jp3_26.pdf

United States Department of State (2002) Patterns of global terrorism. US Department of State, Washington, DC

Viscusi WK, Zeckhauser RJ (2003) Sacrificing civil liberties to reduce terrorism risks. J Risk Uncertain 26(2–3):99–120

Walkenhorst P, Dihel N (2002) The impact of the terrorist attacks of 11 September 2001 on international trading and transport activities. OECD

Zeidan S (2006) Agreeing to disagree: cultural relativism and the difficulty of defining terrorism in a post-9/11 world. Hast Int Comp Law Rev 29(2):215–232

Zussman A, Zussman N (2006) Assassinations: evaluating the effectiveness of an Israeli counterterrorism policy using stock market data. J Econ Perspect 20(2):193–206

Zussman A, Zussman N, Nielsen MØ (2008) Asset market perspectives on the Israeli–Palestinian conflict. Economica 75(297):84–115

Chapter 3
Terrorism as a Mode of Warfare

Abstract Terrorism comprises two aspects: a theory of violence and a strategy of violence perpetrated to achieve a stated goal. Terrorism itself is a strategy—some scholars even describe terrorism as a tactic—of warfare and serves the expression of political discontent but, in turn, contains strategic concepts to achieve an ultimate desire or sub-goals. These concepts can be enforced by employing different tactics.

Terrorism comprises two aspects: a theory of violence and a strategy of violence perpetrated to achieve a stated goal. Terrorism itself is a strategy—some scholars even describe terrorism as a tactic—of warfare and serves the expression of political discontent but, in turn, contains strategic concepts to achieve an ultimate desire or sub-goals. These concepts can be enforced by employing different tactics.

To tackle the problem of the different dimensions of terrorism, Sect. 3.1 considers some implications of strategy and tactics related to terrorism. This is important insofar as the term "strategy," later used in the context of game theory, must be distinguished from a strategy in the military sense.

Section 3.2 discusses the similarities and differences between guerrilla warfare and terrorism as most insurgency groups incorporate both aspects of guerrilla and terrorism. Subsequently, in Sect. 3.3, different strategic concepts are presented, which fall into two categories. Some concepts pursue stated goals and serve political ends. Other concepts serve the almost mundane function of ensuring a terrorist group's survival. Although they are not necessarily mutually exclusive, and terrorists have often espoused them concurrently, these concepts of terrorism are considered separately.

Each approach will be more suitable in some environments than in others. These environments are typically determined by the potential target's regime type, which impacts on the effectiveness of a given strategy. Therefore, critical elements concerning a terror group's choice of target are highlighted and discussed in Sect. 3.4.

© The Author(s), under exclusive license to Springer Nature Switzerland AG 2020

N. Ismael, *Strategic Interaction Between Islamist Terror Groups*, SpringerBriefs in Economics, https://doi.org/10.1007/978-3-030-51307-8_3

3.1 Strategy or Tactics . . . or Whatever

Paraphrasing Carl von Clausewitz (1976 [1832], p. 87), war—and therefore terrorism—is merely a continuation of policy by other means. In this context, policy can be conceived as the decision to take action and perform this act in a particular way, or it can be described as the activities and relationships that influence the formulation of policy. For Clausewitz, the formulation of policy was a matter of judgment, which could be undertaken by both states as well as non-states[1] (Echevarria II 2007, pp. 196–198).

Clausewitz defined war as "*an act of force to compel our enemy to do our will*" (Clausewitz 1976 [1832], p. 75). Terrorism as a mode of warfare is fought by rivals of unequal strength: by states and terrorist organizations and has come to be known as asymmetric warfare (Arreguin-Toft 2001, p. 635). States have access to the military, intelligence, security, and police agencies. They can usually raise substantial funds for and dedicate considerable resources to fighting an enemy. In contrast, terrorist groups have far more limited resources and fewer arms. This asymmetry is reminiscent of the biblical tale of David and Goliath (Fischerkeller 1998, p. 2). Since terrorists are the weaker adversary in terms of means, terrorism inevitably focuses almost exclusively on the will, and the way groups use terrorism is a "strategy" of warfare.

Scholars and strategists have always theorized about the meaning of strategy. Von Clausewitz stated that strategy is the art of using battles to win the war, while tactics are the art of using troops in battle (Clausewitz 1976 [1832], p. 128 and p. 177). Hence, a strategy constrains the tactics used.

Clausewitz's comprehension of strategy and tactics is not only suitable for conventional wars but is also applicable to terrorism. Then, terrorism itself is a strategy that uses attacks to attain an ultimate goal. Strategic concepts of terrorism, likewise, specify this goal. Terrorist groups, which deploy terrorist foot soldiers, weapons, finances, and other material, use tactics that range from assassination, armed assaults, and kidnappings to hijackings and explosives, including suicide bombings. Figure 3.1 provides an overview of the attack types used by terrorist groups[2] for the period between 1985 and 2016.

---

[1]Clausewitz refers to the Tatar tribes, which originated in Central Asia and participated in Mongol invasions in eastern Europe and the Middle East. Furthermore, they are assumed to had converted to Islam and joined in Ottoman jihads against the West (Benson 1981, p. 235). Based on the idea of Hobbesian tribal wars, whose overcoming provides a legitimization of a nation-state and its monopoly of violence, some argue that tribal societies fall outside the Western nation-state paradigm, and, therefore, the example, of the Tatar used by Clausewitz provides an instance of non-state actors (see, among others, Echevarria II 2007, p. 206).

[2]Of course, these types of attack are not exclusive to terrorism and are also employed by other modes of warfare.

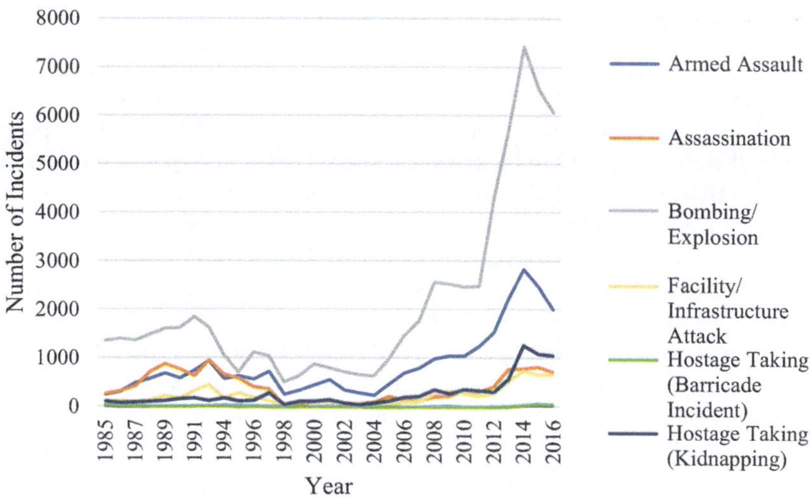

Fig. 3.1 Attack Types, 1985–2016. Source: Global Terrorism Database. Notes: The Global Terrorism Database gathers nine categories of attack types, but only seven are considered here. Attacks, for which the type could not be determined, as well as unarmed assaults (attacks by means other than explosive, firearm, incendiary, or sharp instrument) and hijackings due to their minimal number, were excluded

Globally, bombings and explosions, including improvised explosive devices, are the most common attack type followed by armed assaults. However, when an attack involved explosive devices along with firearms, incendiaries, or sharp objects, the attacks are coded as an armed assault (GTD Codebook 2017). Hence, there is a systematic underestimation of the preferred attack type.

Hostage-taking incidents are subdivided into barricade incidents and kidnappings. The latter involves moving and holding the hostages in another location, whereas the barricade incidents occur and play out at the target location with little or no intention to hold the hostages for an extended period (GTD Codebook 2017).

The peaks can be partly assigned to different events that are characterized by increased terrorist activity, such as the first (1987–1993) and the beginning of the second (2000) *intifada*, the aftermath of the invasion of Iraq, and *Daesh's* momentum in Syria (2014).

In the light of von Clausewitz's explanations, the dimensions of strategy and tactics appear to be obvious. However, a military strategy regularly ignores the opponent's actions, while game theory—the tool used during this thesis—models the strategic interactions of players. Even to military planners, the distinction of military strategy and tactics seems to be ambiguous. As from now, "strategy" refers to the game-theoretic interpretation of any course of action and does not distinguish between strategy and tactics in a military sense.

3.2 Guerrilla Warfare and Terrorism

A kidnapping to exact ransom money is merely a criminal act, when the kidnappers are not pursuing or financing a political end. If it is tied to a political purpose, however, then it is assumed to be terrorism. Boko Haram, a Nigerian-based terrorist group, for instance, kidnapped more than 200 female students in April 2014 to extort the release of Boko Haram fighters from prison. Other prominent examples are the kidnappings of James Foley or Kayla Mueller by *Daesh*. Both groups used kidnappings to enforce their political agendas. Rampages without political intention on, for instance, students and teachers are criminal actions. The hijacking of a commercial airliner by a deranged person is a crime. However, 9/11 and Pan Am Flight 103 both had a political end, which classifies both as acts of terrorism (Sandler 2014).

The differentiation between terrorism and crimes is basically determined by the presence of political purposes. A clear distinction between terrorism and guerrilla warfare poses a greater challenge.

Guerilla warfare generally comprises a band of rebel groups, which controls a sector of a country to take advantage of terrain, from which to dispatch its operatives to confront the enemy force. The physical control of territory provides guerillas with a reservoir for recruitment and infrastructure. Guerilla warfare avoids direct, decisive battles but consist of many small clashes instead and is intended to prevent state forces from employing their full strength. The advantage of terrain enables the guerilla groups to combat small units of government forces against, which they usually fight. Compared to conventional forces, guerillas are inferior in manpower, equipment, and arms but compensate for this inferiority through surprise, secrecy, and hit-and-run tactics[3] to weaken the numerically superior forces of the state. Nevertheless, guerrilla groups conduct warfare like conventional armies. When guerrillas stage an ambush or attack a village, they do it in the same way that a regular infantry unit would (Valentino et al. 2004, pp. 376–378).

Apart from the establishment of territorial control, the military force-like organization distinguishes terrorism from guerrilla (Valentino et al. 2004, p. 384). Terrorism lacks the material elements of guerrilla warfare and remains in the domain of psychological influence (Wilkinson 1977, p. 110). Other differences relate to the unit size, arms, and types of operations, which have their foundations in the military orientation of guerrillas.

However, some guerrilla groups engage in terrorist attacks to raise funds to secure their operations and to pursue their political aims. Consequently, many guerrilla groups are listed as terrorist groups. Also, terrorist groups can use guerilla tactics, which makes the distinction even fuzzier (Byman 2005, p. 26). *Al-Qaeda*, for example, is treated as a terrorist group. Nevertheless, as Osama bin Laden explained in November 2004 *al-Qaeda* "*gained experience in guerrilla warfare [...].*"[4] The

[3]The tactic implies to "hit" the enemy, inflicting damage, and 'run' before the opponent can retaliate.

[4]Al-Jazeera videotape transcript, 2004.

same is true for *Daesh*, which had seized territorial control in Syria but also imposed its will on the general population by sowing fear.

In the case of terrorism, violence is used mainly against noncombatants, although not exclusively, with the intention of reaching a larger audience, and is meant to help achieve a usually political goal. Guerillas direct force toward state forces in a war limited to a particular area.

Although the theoretical and empirical literature puts much effort into drawing a line between guerrilla and terrorist groups, in many instances, the actors involved are often insurgencies that regularly use terrorism (Byman 2005, p. 26). Only in rare cases, an explicit distinction between the two types is constructive. In particular, the recent wave of Islamic-jihadist groups blurs lines. Whereas the key actors in conflict are variably referred to as dissidents, rebels, insurgents, terrorists, and revolutionaries, among other terms, and are often treated separately, they follow a similar objective in their choices to use violence (Findley and Young 2012b, p. 287).

This thesis allows for a range of motivations as well as for terrorist incidents against combatants. To that effect, it also covers attacks conducted in war theaters that are not primarily intended to fight a regular force but to address a broader audience.

3.3 The "Strategies" of Terrorism

To attain their goals, terrorist groups must provide credible information to the resonant mass and promote themselves to potential supporters to signal that they are eligible (Kydd and Walter 2006, p. 58).

Terrorist organizations pursue goals that come in two dimensions: so-called outcome goals and process goals (Abrahms 2012, p. 367). A terrorist group's outcome goal is their stated political objective, for example, the removal of a government, the establishment of an Islamic State, other policy changes, or the maintenance of the status quo. Obtaining these outcome goals depends on the behavior of the terrorists' counterparts, primarily the targeted government. Process or organizational goals, by contrast, aim to ensure survival and sustainability by attracting new members and maintaining support or at least by deterring people to abandon them (Abrahms 2012, p. 367). For this purpose, governmental compliance is not necessarily needed.

Over the years, scholars have suggested several mechanisms, through which terrorism is thought to work. For this thesis, the most fruitful contribution stems from Kydd and Walter (2006), who interpret the ways used by terrorists as costly signals and are therefore most suitable, when it comes to analyzing rivalry between terrorist groups.

The procedures of terrorism identified by Kydd and Walter (2006, p. 51) include attrition, spoiling, provocation, intimidation, and outbidding. While Kydd and Walter refer to all five mechanisms as "strategies," they are qualitatively different. The first four are instruments, which describe how terrorist groups behave, while only outbidding, incorporates strategic aspects in game-theoretical terms, and therefore is of a different character. Similarly, advertising, which has regularly been suggested to be a mediating driver of terrorist activity must also be considered (Goodwin 2006, p. 2038).

3.3.1 Attrition

The most challenging task for any terrorist group is to convince the targeted government that the organization is strong and resolute enough to inflict serious costs so that the government grants concessions over policy or territory. Attrition comprises a constant stream of attacks, which inflicts casualties, destroys properties, and slowly wears down the other side, morally or physically (Arreguin-Toft 2001, p. 105).

Generally, attrition seeks to erode the combat power of the enemy's forces gradually. Bartholomees Jr. (2010) refers to this aspect of attrition as physical attrition, which uses direct attacks against an enemy's forces. However, terrorism does not intend to physically wear down a foe but instead erodes the will to resist over time indirectly, by persuading an enemy's audience to show that resistance will only lead to more casualties (Bartholomees Jr. 2010, pp. 9–10).

Pape (2005) presents the most convincing explanation of terrorism as a war of attrition. Based on a dataset of all suicide attacks from 1980 to 2003 (315 in total), he argues that suicide terrorism is employed by weak actors, for whom peaceful tactics have failed and conventional military tactics are unfeasible because of the imbalance of power (Pape 2005, p. 15).

Starting in July 1990, the *Liberation Tigers of Tamil Eelam* began a series of suicide attacks against Sri Lankan political leaders, military targets, and civilians, as well as using a suicide attacker to kill former prime minister Rajiv Gandhi. Suicide terrorism also spread to Israel in 1994, when the Palestinian terrorist groups *Hamas*, *Islamic Jihad*, and *Fatah* started to use suicide attacks against Israeli civilians and troops (Bloom 2004, p. 70). In 2001 alone, *Hamas* was held responsible for 17 suicide attacks inflicting 69 casualties (Pape 2005, p. 261).

3.3.2 Spoiling

Particularly for civil war situations, policymakers view peace negotiations and conciliations as universal remedies and assume that every civil war is negotiable. Addressing the needs of all warring parties is assumed to lead to a solution, and negotiated settlements are believed to be morally preferable to a (military) victory by one side (Stedman 1997, p. 5).

Whenever two or more sides engage in peace negotiations, there is uncertainty about whether the sides adhere to the settlement. During the negotiation process, there is a natural distrust regarding the motives and intentions of the actors involved. Even if each party sticks to its commitments, it can never be sure the other will as well. It may happen that the former enemy will breach the agreement and send the parties back to war (Kydd and Walter 2002, p. 264).

A spoiling strategy is designed to destroy or at least disturb peace negotiations, which present a danger for a more extreme group or an extreme wing of one of the bargaining partners (Mishal and Sela 2000, p. 103). Terrorist groups exploit natural skepticism by launching attacks sowing mistrust between the negotiating groups, thereby sabotaging the negotiations (Stedman 1997, p. 5).

Spoiling aims to convince the enemy, with whom moderates negotiate that they are not trustworthy, leading to doubts about whether moderates can commit to a peace settlement and are able, or even willing, to stop terrorism (Kydd and Walter 2002, p. 264). A prominent example of successfully bringing down a peace process is the Israeli–Palestinian conflict and the Oslo Peace Process that lasted from 1993 to 2001 and was derailed by *Hamas*. Also, other bargaining processes in the past were characterized by spoiling. The deadly bombing in August 1998 by the *Real IRA*, an offshoot of the *IRA*, was an attempt to halt the peace process and to prevent the Good Friday Agreement from coming into effect.

3.3.3 Provocation

The goal of provocation[5] is to force the enemy into an indiscriminate military response. Disproportional countermeasures can convince the population that the target is untrustworthy and evil (Crenshaw 1981, p. 387). Terrorists try to change the beliefs and preferences of a population by uncovering the repressive attitude of a state (Lake 2002, p. 16).

The provocation of an enemy's overreaction uses the strength of a superior power against itself and can either undermine public support for the government or increase sympathy within the terrorist group's home population.[6] As Fromkin notes, terrorism "*can also make heroes out of gunmen*" (1975, p. 686).

The attacks of 9/11 can be partly interpreted in the light of provocation: bin Laden provoked a massive retaliation by the United States against Islamic countries, thereby allegedly revealing for all Muslims the imperialist and anti-Islamic face of the United States. Suffering under US military assaults, moderates in the Arab world would then come to see the United States as the extremists see them and would ally with the extremists, thereby increasing their numbers and power (Lake 2002, p. 20).

---

[5]Fromkin (1975) argues that terrorist behavior always aims to provoke a reaction.

[6]The provocation of disproportional state repression can also have the opposite effect. By attacking civilians, terrorist attacks facilitate the justification of draconian measures by the government. Furthermore, there is always the risk that the population that terrorists seek to convince will end up blaming the group for causing repression and harm (Thornton 1964, p. 53; Bueno de Mesquita and Dickson 2007, p. 375).

Lake argues that a deliberate provocation would not only drive people into the arms of a terrorist group and radicalize moderates but also provide information about the type—hawk or dove—of government. For moderates, this information is crucial in peace process negotiations and shows how the government will likely behave (2002, pp. 19–20). Bueno de Mesquita and Dickson (2007, p. 371) further note that a disproportional response, even though an adequate one might be available, can give the impression that a government is not interested in its citizens' welfare, creating even more support for terrorists (2007, p. 371). This might also apply within the scope of third-party interventions. *Jabhat Fateh al-Sham*, for instance, is expected to benefit in Syria concerning acceptance and support within the Syrian opposition population because it is exploiting the widespread belief that the international community does not care about the suffering of the Syrian population (Lister 2016, p. 6). If a party hesitates due to indecisiveness, reluctance is presented as disregard directed against the population that the organization wishes to manipulate.

3.3.4 Intimidation

Terrorists often compete with governments and other groups for the support of the population. If an organization intends to overthrow or replace a government, it must convince the state's defenders that continued backing will be costly (Kydd and Walter 2006, p. 66). By providing clear evidence that the terrorist organization can and will kill those, who support the government or other targets, terrorist groups gain societal control over a population, or at least parts of it (Findley and Young 2012b, p. 287).

Intimidation serves to demonstrate that terrorist groups have the power to punish, whoever disobeys them and that the government is powerless to stop them. To that effect, intimidation is akin to the strategy of deterrence. It prevents some undesired behavior using threats and costly signals (Kydd and Walter 2006, p. 66).

An intimidation strategy can encompass a range of actions—from assassinations of individuals to suicide bombings either using explosive belts or car bombings. It can also include massacres of civilians, who have cooperated with the government or rival groups. Such massacres are especially common during civil wars in villages that had once been under rebel control but that the military was attempting to retake and clear of rebels (Kalyvas 1999, pp. 251–252).

Intimidation can usually be observed in the context of civil wars or in fragile phases of state building or renewing. *Daesh*, for instance, deployed intimidation tactics in Syria. *The Taliban* in Afghanistan also used coercive behavior to deter citizens from aiding the Americans. During the Vietnam War, the Vietcong displayed its coercive capabilities to punish people, who, they assumed, supported the Americans. Also, the *Shining Path*—a terror organization that intended to establish a Marxist state in Peru—used intimidation during the 1980s and 1990s to ensure compliance (Findley and Young 2012b, p. 297).

Contrary to other mechanisms that seek to persuade civilians to support the group voluntarily, intimidation comprises coercive behavior and forced compliance. The intention to spread fear among an opponent's ranks constitutes the salient psychological element that characterizes terrorism.

3.3.5 Advertising

Advertising does not represent a separate strategy. Rather, it is a means to an end, and its basic idea was phrased as "propaganda by the deed" (Thornton 1964, pp. 82–83; Laqueur 1987, pp. 48–51).

The original concept of propaganda by the deed was more defined than its modern usage, though terrorist attacks were and are employed as a communication strategy and terrorist groups intentionally choose their targets and their timing to gain and maximize media attention (Rohner and Frey 2007, p. 130). Terror attacks often take place in big cities with a high density of press agencies, and they tend to attack before or during big media events, such as elections, international summits, e.g., G8 summits or the Olympic games, to name a few. Although one purpose during political summits is to influence the decision process of the politicians, the violence used also demonstrates, to current and potential supporters, a capacity to deliver blows against their opponents. Media attention, therefore, is an essential vehicle, by which terrorists communicate with their audience (Nacos 2002, p. 105 and p. 186).

However, terrorist attacks differ widely in the amount of media attention they receive. Most terrorist attacks receive little attention from major media outlets. Others, such as those 2001 in New York and Washington, DC, London in 2005, and Mumbai in 2008, received high coverage.

Advertising of the movement's aims can serve a major purpose; especially where symbolic targets are chosen. Furthermore, it is a means of gaining popular support, when attacks will convince sympathizers that the organization is more effective than rival groups in challenging authorities (Chenoweth 2010, p. 21). Additionally, advertising is also crucial for fostering the credibility of a terrorist movement, signaling that it is capable of inflicting substantial harm, when an organization's demands are not satisfied.

Media attention may not only be the consequence of advertising, but it also may involve a terrorist group's attempts to produce and distribute propaganda material through different media channels. Such advertising strategy is practiced and perfected by *Daesh* (or its predecessor *al-Qaeda in Iraq*), which has spent a great deal of effort in promoting its deals through the Internet and social media. The ease in accessing vast potential audiences and the lack of regulation are only some of the advantageous attributes that led to increasing use of "new technologies" by terrorist movements to threaten societies and achieve their goals. Saltman and Winter (2014) emphasize the innovations concerning *Daesh's* usage of the internet. According to them, centralized propaganda, global dissemination of threats, and decentralized messages allow *Daesh* to make a big noise to a broad audience (Saltman and Winter 2014, p. 39).

Apart from the tools, which make propaganda relatively easy compared to how it was in the past, the shock value of the attacks is also important for advertising a group's cause. One of the most common and brutal terror tactics employed by jihadist groups is the beheading of victims[7] and the most well-known figure, Jihadi John, was responsible for a series of beheadings that were publicized due to the footage released to the international media (Wood 2015). Even though these pictures and videos may deter most people, they can inspire certain groups and can draw the media's attention to them.

3.3.6 Outbidding

Outbidding has been particularly emphasized by Bloom, who describes the outbidding strategy as a proliferation of groups in a competitive process (2004, p. 73). With an increasing number of groups vying for endorsement, the shares of resources and support for each group decreases (Bloom 2005, p. 94). Each party attempts to gain support by exceeding the other's professions of loyalty and commitment to the cause (Kydd and Walter 2009, pp. 2–3). Groups competing with each other may, therefore, promote increasingly extreme positions and use increasingly spectacular tactics or engage in high-frequency attacks to attract more support (Kaufman 1996, p. 106).

In addition to the competitive pressures, outbidding likely occurs if groups' preferences are subject to uncertainty. If the population is fully aware of the competing organizations' interests, people would merely support the group, which best fits their preferences. In such a case, outbidding would be pointless. However, the potential constituency can never be sure whether it sympathizes with zealots or sellouts so that there is some risk that a group betrays its interests. In a competitive environment, organizations have an interest to signal that they are strong and decisive, instead of weak and prone to selling out. Terrorist attacks, then, serve as a signal that the group has both the capability and the will, and will also explain why terrorist organizations conduct attacks that do not politically pay off but simply impose costs (Kydd and Walter 2006, p. 76). Kydd and Walter (2009) assume that the combination of uncertainty and competition produces the incentive to engage in competitive attacks, resulting in ever more violence and an "overproduction" of terrorism.

[7]There is no doubt that jihadist beheadings have become more widely known as a result of the Iraq conflict. Campbell (2006, p. 584) notes that there have been increasingly more beheadings occurring worldwide since the first videotaped and publicized beheading in 2002.

The logic underlying outbidding has received much attention within the literature[8] and has been particularly "verified" in the context of suicide terrorism. Bloom illustrates outbidding in the context of Palestinian suicide bombings. She argues that suicide bombings have become a method of recruitment for militant Islamic organizations within the Palestinian community and that the tactic flourished in the Palestinian case due to competition between *Hamas*, *Fatah,* and *Islamic Jihad,* especially with the beginning of the second intifada (Bloom 2005, pp. 89–94). In September 2000, peace negotiations between the Israelis and the Palestinians broke down, bringing to a bitter end the optimism that had greeted the signing of the Oslo Accord 7 years earlier. The Palestinian economy was in ruins, and Ariel Sharon provocatively visited the Temple Mount to reinforce his nationalist credentials. Rioting broke out immediately, and Israel responded aggressively. According to Bloom, this marked the environment, in which various political organizations competed against each other for the leadership of the Palestinian community (Bloom 2005, p. 70). Data show an increase in the number of groups using suicide attacks over time, yet no single group dominated suicide bombings for an extended period. Brym and Araj state that this pattern is consistent with the position that terrorist organizations increasingly used suicide bombings to outbid competitors and garner public support (2008, p. 487). However, they do not find any statistically significant correlation between suicide bombings and popular support of a particular terrorist group using public opinion polls from 2000 to 2004, which incorporated suicide attacks on Israelis and looked at Palestinians' support for Palestinian terrorist groups (Brym and Araj 2008, pp. 488–489).

While support for outbidding in the context of terrorism has been found using limited case study evidence,[9] cross-national validation lacks or suggests scant evidence. Findley and Young (2012a) use data from the GTD from 1970 to 2004 to ascertain a link between terrorism and outbidding. They find minor cross-national evidence concerning the relation of terrorism and outbidding, which, they conclude, indicates that the specificity of cases causes support for outbidding in the context of terrorism, particularly in the Palestinian case (Findley and Young 2012a, p. 719).

Bloom's theory of outbidding highlights the role of competition between violent groups and explains that such groups turn to an extreme form of violence concerning frequency and scope, ending up in a "violence spiral."

In the broadest sense, groups representing the same community vie for the right to claim responsibility for attacks (Bloom 2004, p. 73). Nevertheless, in some instances, no group takes credit for attacks, which would not correspond with the logic of outbidding. Bloom (2005) assumes that some groups avoid claiming responsibility for attacks due to fear of alienating their supporters. If public opinion among supporters condemns the terrorist behavior, then groups are likely to deny their involvement.

---

[8]See, for example, Horowitz (1985), Brym and Araj (2008), and Iyengar (2010) for outbidding in ethnic and political conflict environments.

[9]Besides the above-mentioned Palestinian case, Lilja (2009) investigated the outbidding theory for terrorist behavior in Sri Lanka, Indonesia, and Senegal. In all three case studies, she finds a pattern of outbidding. Boyle (2009) finds support for outbidding in Iraq using data from 2003 to 2008. See also Iyengar (2010) for outbidding in the Iraq case.

3.4 Some Comments on the Choice of Target

Each mechanism of terrorism will be more effective in some circumstances than in others. For example, a spoiling strategy only makes sense in an environment, where negotiations already take place or are in the making, while intimidation may mainly work during times of civil wars.

In addition to these situational conditions, the suitability and success of terrorism are mainly influenced by three factors. Kydd and Walter identify the state's degree of interest in the disputed outcome, the constraints on countermeasures, and the target's willingness to tolerate costs associated with terrorism as driving variables concerning the feasibility of terrorists' strategies (2006, p. 62).

At their heart, these factors are attributable to the regime type, and the effectiveness of the presented strategies mainly depends on the question of how terrorism is affected by a certain regime. Democracies, for example, are assumed to be the preferred targets of groups conducting attritional campaigns such as suicide bombings[10] (Kydd and Walter 2006, p. 63), whereas authoritarian regimes, such as those in Algeria, Iraq, or Syria faced and continue to face campaigns by organizations following an intimidation strategy (Carter 2015, p. 117).

Some have argued that democratic societies offer access for citizens to seek recourse to their grievances, while democratic rules ensure the nonviolent resolution of conflicts of interest. A lack of opportunities for expression of political grievances, then, facilitates terrorism (Crenshaw 1981, p. 383), so dissenters are less likely to resort to terrorist violence for expressing their grievances in societies where freedom of expression is encouraged (Schmid 1992, p. 194). Therefore, democracy is expected to lower the opportunity costs of achieving one's goals through legal means, thereby making terrorism less attractive to would-be perpetrators (Eyerman 1998, p. 161; Li 2005, p. 280). To the extent that democratic participation increases the political efficacy of citizens, terrorist groups will be less successful in recruiting new members in democracies than in autocracies, providing an argument as to why democracies are less targeted by domestic terrorist groups (Li 2005, p. 292). However, while the participation in political processes may discourage domestic terrorism, this does not apply to transnational terrorist groups, which have their roots elsewhere but attack democratic states. These groups neither can nor will participate in democratic norms.

Press freedom, as part and parcel of civil liberties, may positively affect terrorism through two distinct processes. First, and most bothersome to researchers, is the problem of underreporting bias across different regime types (Drakos and Gofas 2006b, p. 137). Autocracies avoid reporting the existence of oppositional violence by restricting media content. The "free" media within a democracy, on the other hand, have an incentive to report both transparently and sensationally (Nacos 2002, p. 47) and the government places fewer restrictions on such media content (Li 2005,

[10]Notwithstanding, most attrition campaigns were usually employed in civil wars, which, in turn, are rooted in countries with less democratic institutions.

p. 158). Since data on terrorism incidents are collected from open sources, the empirical record will likely conclude that democracies more often than not become the target of terrorist incidents. Even if nondemocratic countries experience the same number of attacks, observers may never know about this if relying on data collected from open sources. Reporting bias may thus lead researchers to an erroneous conclusion that civil liberties contribute to terrorist violence (Li and Schaub 2004, p. 29).

Press freedom may have a more direct causal effect on terrorism, however. Sensational media coverage serves the terrorists in their recruiting, teaching, and training techniques. Because of the free press in most democracies, terrorists have increased incentives to grow in, move to, and conduct their violence within such countries, using media coverage to advertise themselves and making democracies as targets more likely.

Moreover, legal systems are less able to quickly pursue and prosecute potential terrorists due to the constraints placed on them by civil rights. Political leaders, for instance, have expressed frustration about the constraining effects of civil liberties in conducting the "war on terrorism": "*the spirited defense of civil liberties is a tactic that aids terrorists [. . .] erodes our national unity [. . .] diminishes our resolve [and] gives ammunition to America's enemies*" (Ashcroft, quoted in Crank and Gregor 2005, p. 158). Li (2005) suggests that the positive effect of civil liberties and press freedom may be only a minor part of a crucial aspect of democratic governance, namely the presence of institutional constraints on the decision-making power of the government. If institutional checks and balances constrain the executive, then state violations of civil liberties should be less frequent (Li 2005, p. 279). A democratic government is thus unlikely to engage in counterterrorism activities that could be perceived as undermining core democratic values. Authoritarian regimes, on the other hand, are less constrained and are more able to find and crush terrorist organizations (Crenshaw 1981, p. 385; Wilkinson 2001, p. 29).

Given these theoretical (and partly empirical) discrepancies, Li (2005) posits that democracy may simultaneously reduce and promote terrorism through different mechanisms. Li finds support for both the democratic participation and the institutional constraints hypotheses, concluding that these features of democracy may have competing effects on the propensity for terrorist groups to attack a regime (2005, p. 279).

To make things more confusing, democratic design, transitions, and policies may also affect the propensity of a state to be attacked (Berrebi and Klor 2006, p. 917; Burgoon 2006, p. 181). That is, it is neither the freest nor the most repressive states, but rather the intermediate states that experience the most terrorism.[11] Ostensibly, democratic transitions are particularly vulnerable events, as a fragile country attempts to overcome the potential backlash of internal and external actors opposing the transition or its implication (Chenoweth 2007; Gleditsch et al. 2002).

---

[11] Empirical evidence is provided by Eyerman (1998), Lai (2003), and Drakos and Gofas (2006a), among others.

With respect to restrictions on countermeasures, institutional constraints due to civil liberties affect the costs paid by terrorists. The more constrained the government is in its use of force, the less costly, for instance, an attrition strategy on the part of the terrorists can be, and the longer the terrorists can hold out in the hopes of achieving their goal. Governments that can absorb heavier costs and hold out for longer are less inviting targets for terrorism. Democracies may be less able to tolerate painful effects of terrorism than non-democracies as citizens will be more likely to demand an end to the incidents. More authoritarian governments exert more control over the media and can disregard public opinion to a greater extent.

However, among democratic states, sensitivity to costs varies with the party or parties in power. When more dovish parties are in charge, the target may be perceived to have lower cost tolerances than if a more hawkish party were in power. A hawkish government, for example, makes spoiling more valuable as they tend to end negotiation processes sooner, while dovish bargaining partners give them more chances (Kydd and Walter 2002, p. 289).

A state's degree of interest in the disputed outcome is less tied to the regime type compared to cost tolerance and institutional constraints. Since democratic states or, essentially, their politicians must interact with the public to maintain political support, a regime with only peripheral interests will be more likely to accede to terrorists' demands. In contrast, states with more important interests at stake rarely do so. The US withdrawal from Lebanon following the bombing of its barracks there is said to be the consequence of marginal interests in maintaining stability and preventing Syrian domination of the country. In this case, the costs of the attack outweighed the US's interests. In contrast, the United States responded to the September 11 attacks by launching offensive wars in Afghanistan and Iraq rather than withdrawing troops from the region, as *al-Qaeda* demanded (Kydd and Walter 2006, p. 61).

References

Abrahms M (2012) The political effectiveness of terrorism revisited. Comp Pol Stud 45(3):366–393

Arreguin-Toft I (2001) How the weak win wars: a theory of asymmetric conflict. Int Secur 26 (1):93–128

Bartholomees JB Jr (2010) The issue of attrition. Parameters 40(1):5–19

Benson DS (1981) The Tartar War. Maverick, Chicago

Berrebi C, Klor EF (2006) On terrorism and electoral outcomes: theory and evidence from the Israeli-Palestinian conflict. J Confl Resolut 50(6):899–925

Bloom MM (2004) Palestinian suicide bombing: Public support, market share, and outbidding. Political Science Quarterly 119(1):61–88

Bloom M (2005) Dying to kill: the allure of suicide terror. Columbia University Press, New York, NY

Boyle MJ (2009) Bargaining, fear, and denial: explaining violence against civilians in Iraq 2004–2007. Terror Polit Violence 21(2):261–287

Brym RJ, Araj B (2008) Palestinian suicide bombing revisited: a critique of the outbidding thesis. Polit Sci Q 123(3):485–500

Bueno de Mesquita E, Dickson ES (2007) The propaganda of the deed: terrorism, counterterrorism, and mobilization. Am J Polit Sci 51(2):364–381
Burgoon B (2006) On welfare and terror: social welfare policies and political-economic roots of terrorism. J Confl Resolut 50(2):176–203
Byman D (2005) Deadly connections: states that sponsor terrorism. Cambridge University Press, New York, NY
Campbell LJ (2006) The use of beheadings by fundamentalist Islam. Global Crime 7(3–4):583–614
Carter D (2015) When terrorism is evidence of state success: securing the state against territorial groups. Oxf Econ Pap 67(1):116–132
Chenoweth E (2007) The inadvertent effects of democracy on terrorist group proliferation. Ph.D. dissertation. University of Colorado at Boulder
Chenoweth E (2010) Democratic competition and terrorist activity. J Polit 72(1):16–30
Crank JP, Gregor P (2005) Counterterrorism after 9/11: justice, security, and ethics reconsidered. Lexis-Nexis, Cincinnati, OH
Crenshaw M (1981) The causes of terrorism. Comp Polit 13(4):379–399
Drakos K, Gofas A (2006a) In search of the average transnational terrorist attack venue. Defence Peace Econ 17(2):73–93
Drakos K, Gofas A (2006b) The devil you know but are afraid to face: underreporting bias and its distorting effects on the study of terrorism. J Confl Resolut 50(5):714–735
Echevarria AJ II (2007) Clausewitz and the nature of the war on terror. In: Strachan H, Herberg-Rothe A (eds) Clausewitz in the twenty-first century. Oxford University Press, Oxford, pp 196–218
Eyerman J (1998) Terrorism and democratic states: soft targets or accessible systems. Int Interact 24 (2):151–170
Findley MG, Young JK (2012a) More combatant groups, more terror?: Empirical tests of an outbidding logic. Terror Polit Violence 24(5):706–721
Findley MG, Young JK (2012b) Terrorism and civil war: a spatial and temporal approach to a conceptual problem. Perspect Polit 10(2):285–305
Fischerkeller MP (1998) David versus Goliath: cultural judgments in asymmetric wars. Secur Stud 7(4):1–43
Fromkin D (1975) The strategy of terrorism. Foreign Aff 53(4):683–698
Gleditsch NP, Walkensteen P et al (2002) Armed conflict 1946–2001: a new dataset. J Peace Res 39 (5):615–637
Global Terrorism Database (2017) Codebook. Accessed 23 Oct 2018. https://www.start.umd.edu/gtd/
Goodwin J (2006) A theory of categorical terrorism. Soc Forces 84(4):2027–2046
Horowitz DL (1985) Ethnic groups in conflict. University of California Press, Berkeley
Iyengar R (2010) The impact of asymmetric information among competing insurgent groups: estimating an 'emboldenment' effect." CEP Discussion Paper No 1018
Kalyvas SN (1999) Wanton and senseless? The logic of massacres in Algeria. Ration Soc 11 (3):243–285
Kaufman SJ (1996) Spiraling to ethnic war: elites, masses, and Moscow in Moldova's civil war. Int Secur 21(2):108–138
Kydd A, Walter BF (2002) Sabotaging the peace: the politics of extremist violence. Int Organ 56 (2):263–296
Kydd AH, Walter BF (2006) The strategies of terrorism. Int Secur 31(1):49–80
Kydd A, Walter B (2009) Outbidding and the overproduction of terrorism. Unpublished manuscript
Lai B (2003) Examining the number of incidents of terrorism within states, 1968–1977. Presented at the annual meeting of the American Political Science Association, Philadelphia
Lake DA (2002) Rational extremism: understanding terrorism in the twenty-first century. Dialogue IO 1(1):15–28
Laqueur W (1987) The age of terrorism. Little, Brown and Company, Boston

Li Q (2005) Does democracy promote or reduce transnational terrorist incidents? J Confl Resolut 49 (2):278–297
Li Q, Schaub D (2004) Economic globalization and transnational terrorist incidents: a pooled time series analysis. J Confl Resolut 48(2):230–258
Lilja J (2009) Trapping constituents or winning hearts and minds? Rebel strategies to attain constituent support in Sri Lanka. Terror Polit Violence 21(2):306–326
Lister C (2016) Profiling Jabhat al-Nusra. Brookings Institution, Washington, DC
Mishal S, Sela A (2000) The Palestinian Hamas: vision, violence, and coexistence. Columbia University Press, New York
Nacos B (2002) Mass-mediated terrorism: the central role of the media in terrorism and counterterrorism. Rowman-Littlefield, Boulder, CO
Pape RA (2005) Dying to win: the strategic logic of suicide terrorism. Random House, New York
Rohner D, Frey BS (2007) Blood and ink! The common-interest-game between terrorists and the media. Public Choice 133(1–2):129–145
Saltman EM, Winter C (2014) Islamic state: the changing face of modern Jihadism. Quilliam Foundation, London
Sandler T (2014) Terrorism and counterterrorism: an overview. Oxf Econ Pap 67(1):1–20
Schmid A (1992) Terrorism and democracy. Terror Polit Violence 4(4):14–25
Stedman SJ (1997) Spoiler problems in peace processes. Int Secur 22(2):5–53
Thornton TP (1964) Terror as a weapon of political agitation. In: Eckstein H (ed) Internal war: problems and approaches. Free Press, New York, pp 71–99
Valentino B, Huth P, Balch-Lindsay D (2004) Draining the sea: mass killing and guerrilla warfare. Int Organ 58(2):375–407
Von Clausewitz C (1976 [1832]) On war. Princeton University Press, Princeton, NJ
Wilkinson P (1977) Internal terrorism and the liberal state. In: Terrorism and the liberal state. Palgrave, London
Wilkinson P (2001) Terrorism versus democracy: the liberal state response. Frank Cass, London
Wood G (2015) What ISIS really wants. The Atlantic 315(2):78–94

Chapter 4
The Economics of Terrorism

Abstract Not only because of but mainly since the attacks on September 11th in 2001 by *al-Qaeda*, political scientists and economists have made increased contributions to the study of terrorism. By doing this, economists treat terrorism as an economic phenomenon and apply economic principles to terrorist behavior.

Not only because of but mainly since the attacks on September 11th in 2001 by *al-Qaeda*, political scientists and economists have made increased contributions to the study of terrorism. By doing this, economists treat terrorism as an economic phenomenon and apply economic principles to terrorist behavior.

One feature in the relationship of terrorist organizations and their counterparts lies in the nature of asymmetric information because targets, e.g., states or governmental institutions, usually do not have information or are ill-informed concerning the capacities of terrorist organizations (Overgaard 1994), while terrorists are better informed about their adversaries' capabilities. This information asymmetry provides terrorist organizations with an information advantage, which positions them to exploit existing weaknesses.

While governments offer many targets and "*have to be fortunate on a daily basis*" (Sandler 2005, p. 79) due to the terrorists' ability to attack anywhere and anytime (Rapoport 2004, p. 59), terrorist organizations have to be "lucky" only once and avoid losing (Hoffman 2006, p. 52), which provides an advantage to the otherwise weak terrorists, and has been described as the paradox of power (Hirshleifer 1991).

Economic theory, such as rational choice and game theory, highlights the purposefulness and rationality by revealing the strategic nature of terrorism and providing a complementary perspective to approaching the threat of terror organizations. To that end, terrorists and their adversaries are viewed as economic agents, who attempt to maximize their payoff.

Rational-choice models assert how terrorists react to policy-induced changes to their constraints and how governments are apt to respond to terrorist-induced changes. Game theory captures strategic interactions between two or more players. As such, actions are interdependent, and rational actors try to act according to how they think their counterparts will act and react. These interactions can occur between terrorist organizations, terrorists and governments, and among targeted

© The Author(s), under exclusive license to Springer Nature Switzerland AG 2020

N. Ismael, *Strategic Interaction Between Islamist Terror Groups*, SpringerBriefs in Economics, https://doi.org/10.1007/978-3-030-51307-8_4

governments. In the context of terrorism, other actors may also incorporate the media, voters, or the support base that terrorist organizations want to attract.

The purpose of this chapter is to provide an overview of what economics can add to the study on terrorism. Because the application of economic tools assumes rationality, the arguments for why terrorist groups can be treated as economic agents are addressed, and counter-arguments are refuted, making a claim that terrorist groups are rational, and economic methods are appropriate for analyzing terrorism.

The focus of attention within the economic literature of terrorism has been on the effective use of countermeasures. The mainly game-theoretical analysis highlights the necessity of cooperation among governments, when it comes to the question of how to fight terrorism. By exemplifying the aspects of offensive and defensive countermeasures in Sect. 4.2, the pitfalls of cooperation on the part of the governments are demonstrated. Further aspects of any terrorist–government interaction include the already mentioned asymmetries and their impact on negotiation processes.

Section 4.3 examines the critical aspects of competition between terrorist organizations. These competitive facets lay the foundation for a strategic treatment of rival terrorist groups that have been addressed both empirically and anecdotally but lack a model-theoretical analysis.

4.1 Terrorism and Rationality: A Contradiction?

The dominant paradigm in economics is rationality, and economists analyze markets and their participants under the assumption of rational behavior; that is, an actor engaging in economic activity is supposed to be a *homo economicus*, who is assumed to maximize his or her objective function, i.e., a utility function, subject to the constraints that the individual faces.

A rational actor will identify and evaluate the alternatives and their consequences. By calculating the benefits and costs of available options the actor then chooses the option that maximizes his or her benefit, or, if there is uncertainty concerning the outcome, selects the alternative with the highest expected utility (Morgenstern and Von Neumann 1944).

In all cases, the postulate of rationality per se has been regarded as very strict, leading to harsh criticism on the assumed *homo economicus* in real-world settings. Behavior and choice may prove to be ineffective due to missing or incorrect information, incorrect perceptions, and unpredictability, all of which limit rationality. Simon (1972) implemented the concept of "bounded rationality" to account for the fact that perfectly rational decisions are usually not feasible in practice. Individuals use heuristics instead of strict optimization rules to make decisions. Doing so may lead to suboptimal choices that appear to be "good enough" (Simon 1972, p. 176).

Apart from the basic discussion on whether agents do or do not act rationally, the issue appears to become particularly problematic, when applying economic methods and game theory to terrorism. This circumstance is fortified, when suicide terrorism is considered.

However, the concept of rationality has been much misunderstood in the context of terrorism. It is not about how terrorists' objectives are generated, but the way terrorists implement their convictions, which is rational, i.e., the efficient use of scarce resources to achieve these objectives and an effective response to changes in their constraints, which determine rational behavior. Terrorist groups are rational actors, who given their beliefs choose the location, timing, and mode of attack to maximize their benefits attached to an incident subject to a set of constraints they encounter. These constraints include financial, logistical, and organizational aspects such as production costs, labor, institutional, and other resources available to terrorists (Sandler and Arce 2007).

Arguably, in the case of terrorism, the structure of a standard economic utility function must be modified to include satisfaction and intangible rewards to account, for example, for expected rewards in the afterlife. This is especially relevant to religiously motivated terrorism.

Although not every terrorist attack is caused by religious motives, religion is a prevalent driver of today's terrorist organizations, raising even more doubts concerning the rationality of terrorist groups. However, it also provides an example of how an apparently irrational behavior can be interpreted as rational. It is this religious ideology that serves as a heuristic device to calculate benefits and costs associated with actions. Individuals, who follow the path of salvation value martyrdom higher than their potential death (Wiktorowicz and Kaltenthaler 2006, p. 295). Moreover, it is known that terrorist group members and their families are financially compensated and enjoy social welfare benefits (Iannaccone and Berman 2006). Evidence suggests that under the regime of Saddam Hussein, relatives of suicide terrorists were rewarded with US$ 25,000 and families, who lost a terrorist organization member in more regular battleground engagements, were reported to receive US$ 10,000 (Enders and Sandler 2012, p. 156). Therefore, it is reasonable to believe that terrorist group members are also motivated by financial gains.

Given this, it seems as though terrorist attacks result from rational behavior; and it is because of personal convictions that even suicide bombers will believe that the benefits exceed the costs and that the suicide option may be of higher value than the alternatives. Hence, engaging in risky, even deadly, activities is not indicative of irrationality (Sandler and Enders 2007, p. 289).

The pre-9/11 era is characterized in that governments primarily attempted to increase costs by implementing so-called passive or defensive security measures. The installation of metal detectors at domestic airports in January 1973 serves as an example for the purpose to increase the costs for hijackings on the part of the terrorists. Between 1968 and 1972, 124 US and 174 non-US hijackings occurred (Landes 1978). Landes (1978) shows that the mandatory pre-boarding searches of passengers and luggage resulted in significant reductions in aircraft hijackings after 1973. Making one method more costly, however, induced the terrorists to change their behavior and to reallocate their resources toward other targets and modes. The installation of metal detectors led to minor hijacking incidents, but terrorists began to attack US embassies instead. A doubling of US embassy security budgets in 1976 allowed for intensified embassy protections and made it harder for terrorists to attack so they instead started to attack diplomatic personnel instead of properties, leading to increased efforts to secure diplomatic personnel globally. As US interests abroad were secured, terrorists then switched their focus to the US mainland (Cauley and Im 1988).

Enders and Sandler (1993) also estimate the effects of US counterterrorism policies and confirm the findings of Landes. Moreover, their study highlights the policy-induced substitution on the part of terrorist groups. US government action, therefore, led to a change in terrorists' product mix by substituting attack modes, targets, and the location of attacks. Imposing restrictions on terror organizations regarding cost increases for illegal behavior will inevitably induce a reaction on the part of the terrorists.

Governmental action triggering a substitution effect is precisely what choice-theoretic models would predict. Increasing the costs for attacks is similar to changing relative prices in economics. An increase in costs for one attack mode may result in a lower net utility but may enhance alternative attack modes as terrorists tend to switch to less costly attacks.

Active or offensive measures affect the reward side of terrorism and are intended to impact the budget constraints that terrorist groups face by reducing future revenue streams or hitting actual capabilities (Sandler and Arce 2007). Both modes of governmental action are expected to lead to reduced output. Terrorists are capable of taking reactionary measures to find new sources of revenue or ways to lower the costs of their attacks. In order to raise (monetary) rewards, terrorist organizations use a tool of sources that are both legal and illegal.

Moreover, terrorist organizations can wait for governmental enforcement to decline, so that they can change the timing of their attacks. There is empirical evidence for the cyclical pattern of terrorist incidents and the implementation of counterterrorism measures (Sandler and Enders 2004).

Finally, terror groups have been shown to improve the efficiency of their operations. They can benefit from economies of scale and scope if groups share their fixed costs across more types of attacks or by sharing fixed costs of planning across a greater terror offensive over a given period. This is particularly the case, when terrorist organizations are organized as a network operating in various areas, such as *al-Qaeda*. Furthermore, economies of learning can be achieved, when a successful attack by one organization signals to other groups what works. This fact has been understood to be the driving factor for suicide terrorism and its subsequent successes (Bloom 2004).

One argument challenging the paradigm of a rational terrorist, which deserves particular attention, is that terrorism is rarely successful.[1] Abrahms (2006a, b), for

[1]Note that success is determined by granting concessions and achieving stated objectives in this case. It does not relate to logistical success. For criticism concerning the success of terrorism see, among others Wilkinson (1986), Held (1991), Cronin (2009).

example, finds that terrorist organizations targeting military personnel often achieve their political goals at least partially. In contrast, campaigns that focus on civilian targets regularly fail to lead to major political concessions, motivating Abrahms to suggest that terrorism is not successful.[2]

Dershowitz (2002, p. 86) argues that the Palestinian case provides an example of successful terrorism and that Palestinian gains provide evidence for the efficacy of terrorism. Moreover, the Madrid train station bombings shortly before the prime ministerial election in Spain are believed to have had significant influence on the election of José Luis Rodríguez Zapatero, who pledged to end Spanish participation in Iraq and, after his election, began the withdrawal (Rose et al. 2007, p. 187).

Nevertheless, it is often argued that a lack of success is a signal of terrorists' irrationality because terrorist groups repeatedly make mistakes. Rationality, however, requires that actors' beliefs are, on average, correct, i.e., they have rational expectations (Pesaran 1987; Sheffrin 1996). An agent, who makes the same mistake over and over again, is therefore irrational.

Whether successful or not in achieving demands, success is a weak indicator of rationality. Even if terrorist campaigns fail to achieve their stated goals, the groups may value alternatives such as maintaining the status quo, peaceful protests, or participation in the political process less than violent attacks that miss their objectives. Hence, a lack of terrorist incidents' success does not necessarily signal that groups make repeated mistakes, but that the alternatives are worse.

Moreover, in evaluating rationality, terrorists' perceptions concerning the success of a campaign may not be driven by what Abrahms (2006a, p. 46) calls outcome goals, but by process goals that pursue attaining resources in terms of human capital and materials, so that groups benefit even though campaigns appear to be ineffective (Gambill 1998, p. 61). To that effect, terrorism can then be shown to be an entirely rational choice.

Terror groups figure out how best to achieve their purposes given their available resources and hindrances. Efforts to reduce terrorism and to fight terrorist groups by whatever mode will result in incentives to innovate, increase productivity, and substitute on the part of the terrorists. To some degree, these behaviors have been observed in the past and maybe anticipated in the future. All of these processes conform to basic economic principles and show rational responses to changes in terrorists' constraints. Although the ability to rationally weigh out costs and benefits on the part of the terrorist organizations will be continuously challenging, historical, and conceptual arguments support the notion of (expected) utility maximizing terrorists.

---

[2]Like most of the scholars, Abrahms emphasizes that terrorist groups particularly target civilians (2006a, p. 42).

4.2 Countermeasures

A lot of emphases has been put on the analysis of countermeasures, particularly on interactions between two at-risk governments. In general, countermeasures are intended to mitigate the threat of terrorism and avoid incidents. When an attack occurs, they will diminish the consequences of a particular terrorist attack.

As mentioned, countermeasures come in two ways, by offensive or defensive means. The latter increases the costs on the part of the terrorists and are intended to deter an attack. In addition, defensive countermeasures reduce the likelihood of a terrorist group's success and, even if successful, may limit the resulting losses. Protective actions may involve metal detectors and other technological barriers at airports, securing borders, increasing surveillance, and hardening targets in general (Sandler and Siqueira 2006, p. 1371).

Defensive actions transfer the threat to softer targets. In the context of transnational terrorism, the terror threat may be deflected toward other countries, thereby imposing costs on others. Other countries, in turn, can do the same thing, which will increase costs. Furthermore, an actor, who engages in deterrence does not only have to spend resources to protect the homeland and being a less attractive target for potential terrorists but may also suffer costs from the negative external effect, when own properties or people become targeted abroad (Arce and Sandler 2005, p. 185).

In contrast, offensive measures target the terrorist group or its sponsor directly and include actions such as infiltration, preemptive or retaliatory strikes, or freezing assets, thereby making everyone safer, who may be at risk due to the weakened terrorist group. The offensive measure's outcome is a public good, potentially involving a free-rider problem if offensive measures require coordination among several at-risk countries (Sandler and Arce 2003, p. 324).

If, for example, one country was to take the lead in pursuing unilateral offensive action, it would bear the full costs of a military strike, while others would benefit once the threat is removed without carrying any costs so that it has no incentive to share the costs associated with the military raid. One nation will only take action if its benefits exceed the costs, regardless of whether others benefit. If the benefits are assumed to be too small, i.e., smaller than the private costs of offensive action, then a unilateral strike by, for example, the United States will not happen.

To illustrate the different properties of defensive and offensive measures, consider the 3×3 game in Fig. 4.1 where two nations can either participate in offensive action, maintain the status quo, or deter a terrorist threat by defensive means. The bold printed 2×2 submatrices display a 2×2 offensive action game at the upper left corner and a 2×2 defensive action game on the bottom right, respectively.

Offensive action will give public benefits B to each nation, while imposing costs of c carried by the country, which pursues offensive means. If only one nation offensively fights the terrorist threat and the other does not, the latter obtains a free-rider benefit of B. However, in case of mutual action, each nation gains cumulative benefits of $2B$ at an individual cost of c. If both nations maintain the status quo the

Fig. 4.1 3 × 3 preemption–deterrence game. Source: Sandler and Arce (2007, p. 784). Notes: In its very basic form, 2B > c > B and C + f > b > C are assumed to hold

Nation A \ Nation B	*Offensive Action*	*Status Quo*	*Defensive Action*
Offensive Action	$2B - c$ $2B - c$	B $B - c$	$B + b - C$ $B - c - f$
Status Quo	$B - c$ B	0 0	$b - C$ $-f$
Defensive Action	$B - c - f$ $B + b - C$	$-f$ $b - C$	$b - C - f$ $b - C - f$

payoff of inactivity is 0, as there are no benefits and no costs from action.[3] If mutual benefits outweigh private costs but benefits of unilateral action are smaller than these costs, the offensive action game will result in a Prisoner's Dilemma with no nation taking action, i.e., maintaining the status quo (Sandler and Arce 2007, pp. 782–784).

In contrast, when considering only the defensive action game, defensive action will give private benefits *b* at private costs *C* but will also impose costs on the other due to the negative external effect associated with defensive measures. This means that defensive actions by one nation will lead to additional costs of *f* for the other country. If private benefits resulting from defensive action are higher than the costs of implementing measures to deter terrorism, while the other does nothing, each country will choose the defensive action and will impose costs on the other. If mutual action leads to a negative payoff, the defensive action game will also result in a Prisoner's Dilemma, with both nations having a dominant strategy for the defensive measure. Defensive efforts by countries facing the same terrorist threat may then create a deterrence race (Sandler 2003, p. 781).

When considered separately, in their most basic form both types of countermeasures lead to a Prisoner's Dilemma, yet differences arise. The offensive action game is nothing more than a public good contribution game where both players desire action but not participating in the dominant strategy, and under-provision is the outcome (Sandler and Arce 2003, p. 325). Collective action will result in too little proactive response as each country tries to free-ride on the actions of other countries.

In the defensive action case, however, maintaining the status quo is desirable, but both potential targets will implement defensive measures to avoid becoming the softer target. Countries, therefore, engage in too much defense resulting in an overprovision of defense (Sandler and Arce 2003, p. 325).

When opposed to each other and leaving the assumptions unchanged, then defensive measures dominate the status quo and the offensive action efforts. This

[3]Note that the payoff of 0 does not incorporate opportunity costs of inactivity. The payoffs displayed solely reflect the benefits and costs directly associated with action.

Table 4.1 Policy choices and associated game forms

Policies	Alternative game forms
Offensive policies	
Preemption or retaliation	Prisoner's dilemma, chicken, coordination, asymmetric dominance
Group infiltration	Prisoner's dilemma, asymmetric dominance
Intelligence	Asymmetric dominance
Defensive policies	Prisoner's dilemma with action

Sandler and Arce (2003, p. 324)

result, among others, may explain why governments usually prefer the implementation of defensive measures over offensive ones.

Of course, within the 2 × 2 submatrices, different results may apply due to different assumptions concerning the relationship of benefits and costs or asymmetries between the players. The alternative game forms for offensive and defensive action games are illustrated in Table 4.1.

What becomes apparent is that, especially in the case of offensive action, almost every scenario can apply, so that the explanatory power is limited to the insight that offensive actions and the players enforcing them, respectively, represent strategic substitutes, whereas defensive measures are strategic complements, as one country's actions encourage those of other countries.

In any case, game-theoretic considerations highlight the pitfalls of international cooperation in the fight against transnational terrorism. For domestic terrorism, all expected costs and benefits are internalized and, thus, countries possess the proper incentives to choose defensive and proactive measures judiciously.

If the only benefit provided by offensive measures is a public benefit, players free-ride on the other's efforts to fight the terrorist threat, and cooperation will be undermined. Lee (1988) considers the additional option of paid-riding. Countries can provide a safe haven to terrorists in exchange for an assurance that the terrorist group will not attack the country, which enables the group to operate with impunity. Such an agreement can foil other countries' efforts to fight the group. Lee shows that the paid-rider option can dominate the cooperative as well as the free-rider strategy, resulting in a Prisoner's Dilemma, in which one country provides sanctuary to a terrorist group, while the other will not take offensive action (Lee 1988, pp. 23–24.).

Another aspect of defensive action in the fight against terrorism has been highlighted by (Kunreuther and Heal 2003; Heal and Kunreuther 2005), who studied the problem structure of interdependent security, where the decision by one player on whether to invest or to not invest in protection will affect the welfare and the incentives of the other players. In their analysis, the risk each player faces is determined not only by an agent's own efforts to limit a catastrophic event but also by those of others to divert disaster, which can be caused by any player, who does not take sufficient protective measures. The catastrophic event can be caused by any player, who does not take sufficient protective measures. In their analysis, (Kunreuther and Heal 2003; Heal and Kunreuther 2005) give the example of airline security where luggage is only screened at departure and, when transferred from one airplane to another, is not screened again. Insufficient screening at the beginning is associated with the risk to transfer explosive baggage to another airline, which then has the risk of a detonating bomb aboard. In December 1988, Pan Am flight 103 exploded over Lockerbie in Scotland due to a bomb hidden in a bag. The luggage had been poorly screened in Malta, placed on board a flight at Frankfurt airport toward London and finally transferred to Pan Am flight 103 at London's Heathrow Airport (Heal and Kunreuther 2005, p. 202). Even though an airline has invested in sufficient measures, there is a high probability that bags will be transferred from one airline to another, and explosive material remains undetected if other airlines fail to invest in a baggage checking system. If airlines realize that their screening efforts may not be enough to limit a catastrophic event, their incentives to invest in security may be reduced, so that in the extreme case, no airline will invest in improved screening techniques or other forms of protection, although all would be better off by implementing the security measures. On the other hand, if an airline believes that others will invest in security measures, it may have an incentive to so as well, so that there may be an equilibrium, in which all players take protective action (Heal and Kunreuther 2005, pp. 206–207).

The authors show that the outcome of interdependent security problems depends on the security costs, the probabilities of a catastrophic event, and the loss in the associated negative externality that a poor screening performance on one airline's part imposes on other airlines. In contrast to a Prisoner's Dilemma, interdependent security problems involve a chance of contagion, which enables an equilibrium with enhanced protection measures because one player can "tip" the system to the preferred equilibrium (Kunreuther and Heal 2003, p. 233).

In addition to the focus on interrelations between governments to fight terrorism, interactions between governments and terrorist groups have been considered in the framework of game theory. Terrorists usually know their strengths and capacities, while governments must speculate on a terrorist organization's resources based on past attacks. If the government knows that the terrorists could possess enough resources and can incur sufficient costs to force the government to accede to the terrorists' demands eventually, then the government's optimal strategy is to comply in order to avoid an attack. On the part of the terrorists, an organization will refrain from an attack or employ all resources if it is aware that it has insufficient resources. In a deterministic environment, the result would be known at the outset of any game because a finite game of perfect information has a unique subgame-perfect equilibrium (Selten 1965).

In an asymmetric information scenario, however, the government is not fully informed about the strength of a terrorist group. Then, a signaling equilibrium may allow a government to limit its expected costs from attacks, although running the risk that acceding to terrorist demands may become more likely (Lapan and Sandler 1993, p. 392).

The scale of an attack can signal whether the government faces a weak or a strong terrorist group and the government can then accommodate its posterior beliefs concerning the resources of the terrorists (Overgaard 1994, p. 458). These updated beliefs permit the government to decide whether to defy or to capitulate.

This consideration requires that governments are principally willing to concede to terrorist demands. However, one of the pillars of US anti-terrorism efforts is to never negotiate with terrorists (U.S. Department of State 2002, p. xii). Not only the United States but also other governments frequently announce that they will never capitulate or concede to demands because accommodating the terrorists may lose electoral support, depending on how the public evaluates the threat of terrorism.

According to a never-capitulate policy, terrorists would never obtain anything and, therefore, would have no incentive to engage in acts, and would, therefore, be forced to enter negotiations. This outcome implicitly assumes that targets keep to their no-negotiation policy and that it is fully credible to the terrorists (Lapan and Sandler 1988, p. 16). Furthermore, it presumes that terrorists only benefit from terrorist attacks if their demands are met (Lapan and Sandler 1988, p. 18). Obviously, these implicit assumptions do not hold in reality. For example, past concessions undermine a target's credibility concerning the compliance of a non-negotiation policy and actors may gain a positive expected payoff from their actions although they will not be successful. Lapan and Sandler (1988) illustrate the difficulties of the never-capitulate policy using an extensive form game where the target first chooses its level of deterrence that determines a terrorist group's probability of success. Given the level of deterrence and the probability of a negotiation's success, a terrorist organization decides whether or not to attack. Lapan and Sandler show that the effectiveness of a never-capitulate policy depends on the amount of deterrence spending to increase the probability of logistical failure, the terrorists' gains being solely tied to the negotiation success, and the government's credibility. Failures to abide by a stated no-concession policy hinge on a time-inconsistency concern, when the perceived short-run gain from concessions appears to be greater than the long-term consequences owing to the value of a given hostage—e.g., CIA agent William Buckley kidnapped on March 16, 1984, in Beirut, who precipitated the Irangate scandal involving the Reagan administration (Lapan and Sandler 1988, p. 16).

4.3 The Facets of Competition in the Context of Terrorism

In general, terrorist organizations must cope with dual pressures: on the one hand, terrorist groups pursue a particular objective, for instance, policy or territorial change, while on the other hand, organizations seek process or organizational goals. Self-preservation is a fundamental concern of all terrorist groups (Krause 2013).

In environments with multiple terrorist groups, organizations must compete for access to a limited pool of resources to sustain themselves and ensure their activities and effectiveness. Blomberg et al. (2011) and Cronin (2009), for example, find that the number of members and the level of popular support is correlated with an organization's longevity. Hence, increasing the supportive mass and, thereby, a group's resources, may increase the likelihood of survival and, in turn, increase chances to achieve their stated goals (Blomberg et al. 2011, p. 459).

Groups use violence because they will not remain relevant without the use of actions and people will not join an organization that does not appear to be active (Lichbach 1995, p. 16). Nevertheless, the literature is ambivalent concerning the question of whether competition between terrorist organizations benefits or detracts from terrorist groups' operations behavior.

Competition may have various facets and can arise within an organization or between different groups. Sometimes, terrorist groups attack each other, and violent competition starts, when a "reactionary" group forms to attack an extant group with opposing political goals. The *Autodefensas* in Colombia, which formed in order to attack the *FARC* and other leftist groups, is an example; loyalist groups in Northern Ireland are another. What seems to be more common, though, is, when multiple terrorist groups claim to represent the same ethnic group. This has been evident between terrorist organizations fighting for Catholics in Northern Ireland, as well as Palestinians, Tamils, Kurds, and other ethnopolitical groups (Phillips 2015).

However, the following discussion concentrates on the rivalry between groups, and the group behavior of those organizations, which do not primarily attack each other but are considered to behave in a competitive manner that nonetheless allows for coexistence.

4.3.1 Faction-Specific Competition

One aspect of competition refers to behavior between different factions within a terrorist organization. As with political parties, terrorist groups incorporate different factions that pursue organization-wide goals but also faction-specific objectives. Siqueira (2005), for example, explores the relationship between the political and militant wings of the same terrorist organization. He assumes that the actions of each faction can generate organization-wide benefits as well as faction-specific benefits, e.g., advertising the cause, or financing. Faction activities may then be characterized to constitute strategic complements if each activity helps generate resources for the other faction and strategically enhances the other, or strategic substitutes, if one faction detracts resources from the other and activities are substitutable.

Siqueira considers four interactive scenarios for militant and political wings—mutually reinforcing actions and strategic complements, mutually interfering actions and strategic substitutes, reinforcing action by the political wing and detracting action by the militants, and reinforcing action by the militants and detracting action by the political wings (Siqueira 2005, p. 222).

For strategic complements, Siqueira establishes that competition between two factions does not necessarily result in increased activity, because independently acting factions tend to engage in less activity than groups whose factions coordinate efforts. He demonstrates that a faction may work at cross-purposes with the organization's goal, when faction-specific gains are sufficiently strong. In such a scenario, a government can exploit this dissent (Siqueira 2005, p. 227). In the case of strategic complements, he shows that countermeasure efforts, which effectively target just a single faction's activities, can also lead to a reduction of the other faction's actions. For strategic substitutes, however, counterterrorism policies that solely address one wing of the organization may increase activities of the other faction (Siqueira 2005, p. 233). Siqueira's consideration provides insight into interrelations, when a terrorist organization comprises factions, whose activities may reinforce or oppose one another's goals.

Sandler and Arce (2003) also recognize that competing factions within a terrorist group can pose problems for conflict resolution. They analyze a bargaining model whereby the government has incomplete information about the distribution of moderates and hardliners within a terror organization. The government faces a tradeoff between the high benefits associated with appeasing violent hardliners and the political costs of doing so. Furthermore, the government knows that both hardliners and moderates will accept an offer that will satisfy hardliners, whereas moderates will accept something less (Sandler and Arce 2003, pp. 322–323).

If the costs of an acceptable offer to hardliners are too high, a smaller offer that only satisfies moderates may lead to adverse selection because only hardliners will remain in the organization, increasing the likelihood of violence. In this way, successful bargaining can end up resulting in increased violence (Sandler and Arce 2003, p. 332).

4.3.2 Cooperation and Alliances

As has been shown, competitive intragroup behavior may have various effects on an organization. However, for this thesis, competition between terrorist groups is the more interesting part. The other side of intergroup-rivalry is that terrorist organizations, like firms, can cooperate and form alliances to share resources and knowledge, train together, or conduct cooperative attacks (Hoffman 2006). Although the relationships between terrorist groups remain puzzling, because there are reasons to expect groups to act in isolation, cooperative behavior, or alliance structures provide some advantages to terrorist groups.

Cooperation between terrorist organizations may arise, when groups can aggregate their strengths in response to a common threat or a common cause, where strategic incentives to collaborate are obvious. With an increasing number of groups engaging in terrorism, governments fighting terrorism must allocate their counterterrorism resources between more groups (Gaibulloev and Sandler 2013). Cooperation may make terrorist organizations more productive, resulting in lower costs for each group and may increase terrorist organizations' longevity (Phillips 2015).

A prominent example is *al-Qaeda*, which has been a participant in many interorganizational connections but also many other terrorist groups have teamed up with other organizations. *Hamas*, for example, has had other terrorist group allies ever since its founding in the 1980s, and the Colombian group *April 19 Movement* cooperated with other Latin American groups (Horowitz 2010, p. 37).

Contrary to governmental cooperation, alliances between terrorist organizations are informal and no legal contracts or institutions to punish uncooperative behavior exist. In this regard, alliance formations among terrorist groups share common characteristics with cartel agreements between firms, and the incentive to align is basically driven by the hope to increase their capabilities (Horowitz and Potter 2013, p. 200).

This, in turn, means that aligning terrorist organizations are confronted with the same problems of cooperation that exist for governments or firms, i.e., groups may have an incentive to free-ride on the efforts of other groups or to exploit others.

If terrorist organizations share the same outcomes and goals, then their activities may have the characteristics—non-excludability and non-rivalry—of a public good. Although an increasing number of groups that share the same goal makes its achievement more likely, it can reduce the incentive to contribute. A group is unwilling to participate in the "provision" because it tends to benefit from others' actions regardless of whether or not it "pays." To that end, the possibility of free-riding would lead to an under-provision of effort necessary to attain the terrorists' goals. This presents a dilemma for those organizations pursuing an outcome goal but also implies less terrorism.

Besides the collective action problem, terrorist organizations may practice extreme free-riding where only one terror organization carries out attacks and the other terrorist organizations commit no attacks but simply claim credit for the incidents, when individual group survival is the fundamental goal. Groups may have an incentive to deviate from agreements to mutually conduct terrorist incidents. If the cooperating partners anticipate that they will benefit from the attacks conducted by others, in an extreme case, no group will end up engaging in terrorist attacks (Bloom 2004, p. 73).

In summary, when the pursuit of terrorist goals is akin to a public good provision, or if the incentive to shirk or to exploit exists, competition may reduce terrorist behavior as the result of a Prisoner's Dilemma. The groups would, therefore, be better off by collaborating with each other (Phillips 2015).

Nevertheless, terrorist groups are said to succeed, when they cooperate with their counterparts instead of facing collective action difficulties, while governments typically fail to take united action against terrorists. Terrorist groups more easily overcome collective action problems because terrorist leaders are tenured for life so that they view their interactions as continuous, with an uncertain endpoint.[4] This means that their effective discount rate from losses sustained from not cooperating is low; thus, they tend to cooperate more (Sandler and Arce 2007, p. 800). Moreover, the terrorists are weak relative to their adversaries and have little choice but to cooperate.

[4]The repetition of games with an unknown endpoint makes cooperative behavior more likely. See Axelrod (1984) for theoretical and empirical considerations on this topic.

In contrast, the government's discount rates are high because office terms are short, and endpoints are frequently certain. Government officials do not put a lot of weight on future payoffs from cooperating, unlike the citizens, whom they represent. Moreover, governments see less need for cooperation because they view themselves as strong compared to terrorists, and often disagree on what groups are considered to be terrorists; for example, many governments do not consider *Hamas* or *Hezbollah* to be terrorist groups.

Through cooperation, terrorists can seek out the weakest link—i.e., the country with the least security—for their next attack and will dispatch their most capable team. Their cooperation allows them to mount the most formidable attack they can. By failing to cooperate, targeted nations will always present attractive soft targets. Thus, terrorists can exploit the government's collective action failures to great advantage. This is particularly true today with some terrorist groups linked together in a global network, with operative and sleeper cells dispersed worldwide.

4.3.3 Outbidding Continued and Differentiation

If group survival is the fundamental objective of each terrorist organization, then, organizations basically compete for support, e.g., financial resources, members, and sympathizers. As Bloom notes "*where there are multiple groups, violence is a technique to gain credibility and win the public relation competition*" (2005, p. 95). The theory of outbidding is built upon the idea that in a competitive environment each terrorist group tries to stay relevant by using violence to gather rewards, and that recruits and resources are drawn to the most active group. Hence, more escalated levels of terrorist incidents demonstrate each group's ability and commitment relative to other organizations, so that outbidding is even more likely, when there is a greater number of actors competing for the same resources (Bloom 2005, p. 94).

The group that can best signal its capability may ensure its own survival as it will gain the most support. In order to communicate their message, terrorists rely heavily on media coverage, and terrorist groups in competitive markets can gain a significant advantage relative to their rivals if they are better able to capture the media's attention (Scott 2001).

Gathering necessary assets, then, is the driver of competitive escalation. By conducting noteworthy attacks, terrorists can demonstrate resolve, that they have the best odds to achieve outcome goals over time, and that they are willing to impose significant costs on the public (Wood 2014, p. 980). This is especially important for terrorist organizations because, contrary to other political movements, which capitalize on past accomplishments to gain support, terrorists must frequently campaign based on future successes.

Moreover, Chai (1993) argues that the most violent groups attract the most violent recruits. So, at least in the short-term, extreme violence serves the important function of increasing recruitment and support among such individuals. There is some evidence that many individuals joining *Daesh* during its momentum phase in 2014 did so precisely because they were using severe violence. These types of recruits are, in turn, more willing to commit extreme acts of violence that may assist a group during periods of increased competition.

The scale and scope of attacks, then, are the criteria, by which terrorist organizations are judged and how the public perceives them (Lake 2002). To that effect, competition significantly affects not only the quantity but also the quality of terrorist behavior.

Conrad and Greene (2015) suggest that terrorist organizations facing competition are encouraged to conduct more shocking and innovative attacks to distinguish their "brand," meaning that the quality of terrorist attacks ensures recruitment and support within the constituency that endorses violence.

The authors argue that public support and recruitment will be less sensitive to a group's achievement of outcome goals, when a group successfully differentiates itself (Conrad and Greene 2015, p. 549). Their idea of terrorist attack differentiation borrows from the concept of product heterogeneity in economics.[5] Heterogeneity of products enables firms to charge higher prices, when compared to homogeneous product competition. Firms that differentiate their products aim to reduce the substitutability by other firms' products (Chamberlin 1933). Consumers are then less sensitive to price increases, competitors' price drops, or other factors. Thus, differentiation may steepen the demand curve so that it is less elastic, when compared to a more homogeneous product market.

For terrorist organizations, more innovative and shocking tactics make the organization less sensitive to ineffectiveness in achieving outcome goals. Differentiation allows an organization to steepen its demand curve, making it less sensitive to changes in the valuation of its product, which Conrad and Greene assume to be the outcome goal (2015, p. 549).

Groups that do not effectively differentiate themselves will have a shallower demand curve. As a result, any perception that a group is weak or has a low chance of success has a greater impact on their ability to gain support and recruits. The use of more extreme attacks might simply reduce the number of substitutes (Conrad and Greene 2015, p. 549).

Terrorist organizations may expect to derive greater utility by focusing on a few high-yield attacks rather than carrying out many attacks with smaller impacts. For example, it is reasonable to argue that all of *al-Qaeda*'s attacks before and following 9/11 did not have the same impact as that single attack. By committing an innovative or shocking method of attack, or by attacking a high-profile target, terrorist organizations should be better able to distinguish themselves in a given marketplace, particularly concerning their competitors. Successful differentiation, therefore, offers a useful tool to mask an organization's failure to achieve its political goals (Conrad and Greene 2015, p. 550).

[5] Conrad and Greene (2015) describe what economists would refer to as "monopolistic competition," although the authors do not use the term.

Hence, competitive pressures are expected to lead either to increased quantity or, when quality is considered, in less but more severe terrorist behavior.

References

Abrahms M (2006a) Why terrorism does not work. Int Secur 31(2):42–78

Abrahms M (2006b) Al Qaeda's scorecard: a progress report on Al Qaeda's objectives. Stud Confl Terror 29(5):509–529

Arce M Daniel G, Sandler T (2005) Counterterrorism: a game-theoretic analysis. J Confl Resolut 49(2):183–200

Axelrod R (1984) The evolution of cooperation. Basic Books, New York

Blomberg SB, Gaibulloev K, Sandler T (2011) Terrorist group survival: ideology, tactics, and base of operations. Public Choice 149(3–4):441–463

Bloom MM (2004) Palestinian suicide bombing: Public support, market share, and outbidding. Political Science Quarterly 119(1):61–88

Bloom M (2005) Dying to kill: the allure of suicide terror. Columbia University Press, New York, NY

Cauley J, Im EI (1988) Intervention policy analysis of skyjackings and other terrorist incidents. Am Econ Rev 78(2):27–31

Chai S-K (1993) An organizational economics theory of antigovernment violence. Comp Polit 26 (1):99–110

Chamberlin EH (1933) The theory of monopolistic competition, 1st edn. Harvard University Press, Cambridge, MA

Conrad J, Greene K (2015) Competition, differentiation, and the severity of terrorist attacks. J Polit 77(2):546–561

Cronin AK (2009) How terrorism ends: understanding the decline and demise of terrorist campaigns. Princeton University Press, Princeton, NJ

Dershowitz A (2002) Why terrorism works: understanding the threat, responding to the challenge. Yale University Press, New Haven, CT

Enders W, Sandler T (1993) The effectiveness of antiterrorism policies: a vector-autoregression-intervention analysis. Am Polit Sci Rev 87(4):829–844

Enders W, Sandler T (2012) The political economy of terrorism, 2nd edn. Cambridge University Press, Cambridge

Gaibulloev K, Sandler T (2013) Determinants of the demise of terrorist organizations. South Econ J 79(4):774–792

Gambill GC (1998) The balance of terror: war by other means in the contemporary middle east. J Palest Stud 28(1):51–66

Heal G, Kunreuther H (2005) IDS models of airline security. J Confl Resolut 49(2):201–217

Held V (1991) Terrorism, rights, and political goals. In: Frey RG, Morris CW (eds) Violence, terrorism, and justice. Cambridge University Press, Cambridge, pp 59–73

Hirshleifer J (1991) The paradox of power. Econ Polit 3(3):177–200

Hoffman B (2006) Inside terrorism. Columbia University Press, New York

Horowitz MC (2010) Nonstate actors and the diffusion of innovation: the case of suicide terrorism. Int Organ 64(1):33–64

Horowitz MC, Potter PBK (2013) Allying to kill: terrorist intergroup cooperation and the consequences for lethality. J Confl Resolut 58(2):199–225

Iannaccone LR, Berman E (2006) Religious extremism: the good, the bad, and the deadly. Public Choice 128(1–2):109–129

Krause P (2013) The political Effectiveness of non-state violence: a two-level framework to transform a deceptive debate. Secur Stud 22(2):259–294

Kunreuther H, Heal G (2003) Interdependent security. J Risk Uncertain 26(2–3):231–249

Lake DA (2002) Rational extremism: understanding terrorism in the twenty-first century. Dialogue IO 1(1):15–28

Landes WM (1978) An economic study of US aircraft hijacking, 1961-1976. J Law Econ 21 (1):1–31

Lapan HE, Sandler T (1988) To bargain or not to bargain: that is the question. Am Econ Rev 78 (2):16–21

Lapan HE, Sandler T (1993) Terrorism and signaling. Eur J Polit Econ 9(3):383–397

Lee DR (1988) Free riding and paid riding in the fight against terrorism. Am Econ Rev 78(2):22–26

Lichbach MI (1995) The Rebel's dilemma. University of Michigan Press, Ann Arbor, MI

Morgenstern O, Von Neumann J (1944) Theory of games and economic behavior. Princeton University Press, Princeton, NJ

Overgaard PB (1994) The scale of terrorist attacks as a signal of resources. J Confl Resolut 38 (3):452–478

Pesaran MH (1987) The limits to rational expectations. Blackwell, Oxford

Phillips B (2015) Enemies with benefits? Violent rivalry and terrorist group longevity. J Peace Res 52(1):62–75

Rapoport DC (2004) Modern terror: the four waves. In: Cronin AK, Ludes JM (eds) Attacking terrorism: elements of a grand strategy. Georgetown University Press, Washington, DC, pp 46–73

Rose W, Murphy R, Abrahms M (2007) Does terrorism ever work? The 2004 Madrid train bombings. Int Secur 32(1):185–192

Sandler T (2003) Collective action and transnational terrorism. World Econ 26(6):779–802

Sandler T (2005) Collective versus unilateral responses to terrorism. Public Choice 124(1–2):75–93

Sandler T, Arce DG (2003) Terrorism and game theory. Simul Gaming 34(3):319–337

Sandler T, Arce DG (2007) Terrorism: a game-theoretic approach. In: Sandler T, Hartley K (eds) Handbook of defense economics vol 2 – Defense in a globalized world. North-Holland, Amsterdam, pp 775–813

Sandler T, Enders W (2004) An economic perspective on transnational terrorism. Eur J Polit Econ 20(2):301–316

Sandler T, Enders W (2007) Applying analytical methods to study terrorism. Int Stud Perspect 8 (3):287–302

Sandler T, Siqueira K (2006) Global terrorism: deterrence versus pre-emption. Can J Econ/Revue Canadienne D'Economique 39(4):1370–1387

Scott JL (2001) Media congestion limits media terrorism. Defence Peace Econ 12(3):215–227

Selten R (1965) Spieltheoretische Behandlung eines Oligopolmodells mit Nachfrageträgheit-Teil I: Bestimmung des dynamischen Preisgleichgewichts. Zeitschrift für die gesamte Staatswissenschaft 121(2):301–324

Sheffrin S (1996) Rational expectations. Cambridge University Press, Cambridge

Simon HA (1972) Theories of bounded rationality. Decis Organ 1(1):161–176

Siqueira K (2005) Political and militant wings within dissident movements and organizations. J Confl Resolut 49(2):218–236

United States Department of State (2002) Patterns of global terrorism. US Department of State, Washington, DC

Wiktorowicz Q, Kaltenthaler K (2006) The rationality of radical Islam. Polit Sci Q 121(2):295–319

Wilkinson P (1986) Terrorism and the liberal state, 2nd edn. Macmillan, London

Wood RM (2014) From loss to looting? Battlefield costs and rebel incentives for violence. Int Organ 68(4):979–999

Chapter 5
Competition Between Homogenous Terrorist Organizations: A General Model

Abstract In general, it is assumed that a competitive environment fosters terrorist activity. Bloom's (2004) outbidding theory as well as the idea of differentiation proposed by Conrad and Greene (2015) suggests that rivalry of terrorist groups either quantitively increases terrorist activity or changes attack behavior qualitatively, resulting in more spectacular events. According to Bloom, a decline in the number of terrorist incidents is merely the result of lacking support. If the support base terrorist groups want to win over refuses terrorism, then organizations tend to reduce their activities instead of trying to outbid each other.

In general, it is assumed that a competitive environment fosters terrorist activity. Bloom's (2004) outbidding theory as well as the idea of differentiation proposed by Conrad and Greene (2015) suggests that rivalry of terrorist groups either quantitively increases terrorist activity or changes attack behavior qualitatively, resulting in more spectacular events. According to Bloom, a decline in the number of terrorist incidents is merely the result of lacking support. If the support base terrorist groups want to win over refuses terrorism, then organizations tend to reduce their activities instead of trying to outbid each other.

In bargaining situations, Siqueira (2005) finds that increased or reduced terrorist behavior between different wings within one group depends on their relation to each other. If these factions are assumed to be strategic complements, factions tend to engage in less terrorist activity when facing countermeasures, while strategic substitutes may show more activity.

Because competition in general and terrorist group rivalry, in particular, is characterized by an interdependency of decision-making, game theory is an appropriate tool to analyze the effects of competition on terrorist activity. The game theory-oriented literature focuses on games between governments in the realm of countermeasures or between terrorist groups and governments in bargaining situations. A consideration of strategic interaction between separate terrorist organizations, though, is missing from the discussion on the effects of rivalry on terrorist group behavior. This chapter aims to develop a game-theoretical model, in which homogenous terrorist groups are competing for support of their causes, and to highlight the role of competition on terrorist activity.

© The Author(s), under exclusive license to Springer Nature Switzerland AG 2020
N. Ismael, *Strategic Interaction Between Islamist Terror Groups*, SpringerBriefs in Economics, https://doi.org/10.1007/978-3-030-51307-8_5

5.1 Building The Model

Evidence found and released by the US Department of Defense after bin Laden's death in 2011 reveals that, despite the absence of 9/11-style attacks in recent years, Islamic-motivated terrorists still want to inflict damage on apostates, and especially on Americans (U.S. Department of Defense 2011). To accomplish this task, terrorists continually improve their techniques, competing with one another to see who can carry out the next 9/11.

Competition on supremacy requires group survival and sustainability. Thus, vying with other organizations for support is indicative for each group's will to take the lead. In vying for rewards such as recruits, media attention, money, and reputation, among others, terrorist groups can choose attack modes that differ in scope and scale, but all serve as a signaling device for an organization's commitment and capability to its cause. The aim is not to directly confront other groups by force and direct attacks against them, but to convince the resonant mass that oneself is the most capable player. This competitive behavior may explain the occurrence of terrorist attacks, although specific political concessions are unlikely to be granted.

Consider the case, in which two groups, once they have decided terrorism is appropriate, can either conduct a small- or large-scale event. Every attack directed against a soft target is said to be a small-scale attack, whereas spectacular events on less easy targets and with many casualties, which ensure global media attention such as 9/11, are referred to as a large-scale attack.

Large-scale incidents are more difficult to plan and accomplish than small-scale attacks in countries with little protection, e.g., other Western countries than the United States, or areas with power vacua such as Syria or Iraq but provide substantially higher rewards. Thus, the effectiveness of a terrorist attack to address its audience to gain support depends on the time, place, and scope of the attack. In this regard, a full range between small and large events exists, and terrorist group support is expected to increase with the scale of an attack.

With each attack, each player receives the associated rewards of R resp. r, where R denotes the rewards for large and r for small incidents with $R > r$. Depending on where the attacks take place, the degree of sensation may vary. There is a fundamental difference between a small-scale attack experienced in Syria or Iraq or in a Western country. However, in comparison to a large-scale activity r is by assumption smaller than R, so, in relative terms, even a small-scale attack in a Western country is considerably exceeded by a 9/11-style attack. Nevertheless, for the subsequent scenarios, it is important to clarify that a small-scale target is presumed to be identic for both groups.

Ostensibly, a 9/11-like attack is far more expensive than a car bombing in Iraq or even a car assassination like that on Westminster Bridge in London. The Sept. 11 attacks were highly sophisticated in their planning and implementation and required substantial financing. Estimates vary between US$ 400,000 and US$ 500,000 with a large share for extensive travel and pilot training (9/11 Commission Report 2004, p. 169).

Generally, the costs of committing terrorist attacks include the acquisition of bomb-making materials and weapons, travel, communication, living, and—if necessary—training. Some tactics are cheaper than others. Simple bombs, for example, are estimated to cost a terror group between \$ 95 and \$ 300 (Besenyo 2017). For vehicle-ramming incidents, the big factor certainly is the cost of the car.

The multipronged terror attacks in Paris, 2015, were likely not to exceed \$ 10,000 (Windrem 2015), and the attack on the London transportation system in 2005 was estimated to have a price tag of \$ 14,000. According to risk analysts, an attack by *Daesh* is expected to have costs of approximately £5000 in Great Britain, with a big part involving travel expenses.[1]

Compared to a small-scale incident, a large-scale attack is more complex, imposing not only higher costs in terms of human capital and time but also higher technical costs to ensure the same probability of success.[2] Denoting small-scale attack costs with c and large-scale event costs with C respectively, $2c < C$ is assumed to hold.

The following situation is modeled as a game that consists of two periods, and each group has a given amount of resources available in order to conduct a terrorist attack by whatever means. However, it is assumed that the obtained payoff at the first stage cannot be reinvested in the subsequent period, so that the resources available to each group can either be split and allocated to two small-scale events, or the groups can entirely concentrate on planning and scheduling a large-scale attack. If one organization plans to commit a large-scale incident, such attack type is presumed to be solely possible at the second stage of the game, taking account of a more detailed and, thus, time-consuming preparation required for a large-scale attack. Hence, conducting a small-scale attack at stage one and a large-scale attack at stage two is not possible.

At the first stage of the game, both players must choose whether they carry out a small-scale event or wait. In the second stage, they have to decide on whether they commit a small-scale attack again, choose a large-scale attack, or do nothing (*wait*).

Although imposing higher costs, a large-scale attack is presumed to yield a higher payoff than a small one, so each group would prefer a large- over a small-scale incident, that is

$$R - C > r - c. \tag{5.1}$$

Additionally, a small-scale attack is assumed to be rewarding, implying

[1] Presentation of the Annual Airey Neave Memorial Book Prize, November 27th, 2018, Royal United Services Institute, London; identity of the source not to be revealed under the "Chatham House Rule."

[2] The cost function is expected to follow the idea of an O-Ring-production function first proposed by Kremer (1993). Analogous to the space shuttle Challenger which exploded due to a temperature-related failure of a small component, an O-Ring, in a production process that consists of several tasks each task must be completed successfully. With increasing complexity of production, actors lose more from potential failures. Hence, a more complex process will be exponentially expensive to guarantee a certain probability of successful completion.

Fig. 5.1 Payoff matrix at stage one

		Group B	
		small	*wait*
Group A	*small*	$\frac{1}{2}r - c$ (A); $\frac{1}{2}r - c$ (B)	$r - c$ (A); 0 (B)
	wait	0 (A); $r - c$ (B)	0 (A); 0 (B)

$$r - c > 0. \tag{5.2}$$

First, each period's payoff matrix is considered independently, and the scenario for period one is depicted in Fig. 5.1. Note that the two following matrices illustrating period one and period two separately do not represent games and merely serve the clarification on the formation of the specific payoffs.

If both groups choose *small* in period one, then media attention or reputation will be split as the media will deal with both events and potential supporters decide which group to back. Hence, they must share *r*, while each must carry costs *c*. For simplicity, it is assumed that players share rewards equally, and the associated payoff can be either positive or negative, i.e.,

$$\frac{1}{2}r - c \gtrless 0. \tag{5.3}$$

Accordingly, a group that solely conducts a small-scale attack, while the other waits and receives nothing, will gain total attention and increase its rewards at costs *c*. Finally, if both groups wait, the expected payoff is zero as no costs occur.

At the second stage, the terrorists can either commit a small-scale attack again, carry out a large-scale event, or wait, which is equivalent to doing nothing. These actions illustrate the prior-mentioned fact that the individual stages cannot be treated as games, because, if this were the case, playing *small* at stage one would reduce the available strategies to only two at stage two, namely *small* and *wait*, due to the assumption made that *large* is solely playable if *wait* is chosen previously. Hence, the depicted payoffs and actions in Fig. 5.2 do not encompass the strategies of the game.

If both decide on *small* in period two, again, they must share *r*, so they are left with $\frac{1}{2}r - c$. The same logic pertains if both organizations plan to conduct a large-scale attack. Imagine that each group conducts a large-scale attack in the United States—for example, one might think of an attack on the Statue of Liberty by one group and an attack at Lincoln Memorial by the other—then the signaling effect to each group's community is expected to be very strong, so it is, contrary to the payoff both groups attain by playing *small*, which is allowed to be positive or negative, conceivable to imagine that

Fig. 5.2 Payoff matrix at stage two

Group A \ Group B	*small*	*large*	*wait*
Small	$\frac{1}{2}r-c$, $\frac{1}{2}r-c$	$r-c$, $R-C$	$r-c$, 0
Large	$R-C$, $r-c$	$\frac{1}{2}R-C$, $\frac{1}{2}R-C$	$R-C$, 0
Wait	0, $r-c$	0, $R-C$	0, 0

$$\frac{1}{2}R - C > 0 \tag{5.4}$$

holds.

At the second stage, if one group carries out a small-scale attack and the other plays *large*, the former obtains a small-scale event's gain $r - c$, while the latter is left with a large-scale attack's gain $R - C$ as both groups operate in different territories with different degree of sensation. A group that chooses *wait* will always have a payoff of zero, whereas the other receives a payoff of $r - c$ if *small* is played, or $R - C$ if it conducts a spectacular attack.

In order to model the complete game and capture the full scope of strategies, total outcomes from each sequence of payoffs must be evaluated. Given the actions at stage one and two, each group's strategies, then, are (*small*, *wait*), (*wait*, *small*), (*small*, *small*), (*wait*, *large*), and (*wait*, *wait*).

By simply summing up the respective outcomes of both matrices, total payoffs can be derived for each sequence of play and consolidated in one game as depicted in Fig. 5.3.

Obviously,

$$\frac{1}{2}r - c < r - c \tag{5.5}$$

and

$$r - 2c < r - c \tag{5.6}$$

hold.

From Eq. (5.2) follows

$$\frac{3}{2}r - 2c > \frac{1}{2}r - c, \tag{5.7}$$

whereas

		Group B				
		small, wait	*wait, small*	*small, small*	*wait, large*	*wait, wait*
Group A	*small, wait*	$\frac{1}{2}r - c$ $\frac{1}{2}r - c$	$r - c$ $r - c$	$\frac{3}{2}r - 2c$ $\frac{1}{2}r - c$	$R - C$ $r - c$	0 $r - c$
	wait, small	$r - c$ $r - c$	$\frac{1}{2}r - c$ $\frac{1}{2}r - c$	$\frac{3}{2}r - 2c$ $\frac{1}{2}r - c$	$R - C$ $r - c$	0 $r - c$
	small, small	$\frac{1}{2}r - c$ $\frac{3}{2}r - 2c$	$\frac{1}{2}r - c$ $\frac{3}{2}r - 2c$	$r - 2c$ $r - 2c$	$R - C$ $2r - 2c$	0 $2r - 2c$
	wait, large	$r - c$ $R - C$	$r - c$ $R - C$	$2r - 2c$ $R - C$	$\frac{1}{2}R - C$ $\frac{1}{2}R - C$	0 $R - C$
	wait, wait	$r - c$ 0	$r - c$ 0	$2r - 2c$ 0	$R - C$ 0	0 0

Fig. 5.3 The complete game

		Group B	
		small, small	*wait, large*
Group A	*small, small*	$r - 2c$ $r - 2c$	$R - C$ $2r - 2c$
	wait, large	$2r - 2c$ $R - C$	$\frac{1}{2}R - C$ $\frac{1}{2}R - C$

Fig. 5.4 The reduced game

$$r - 2c \gtrless \frac{1}{2}r - c \tag{5.8}$$

is determined by Eq. (5.3).

Cell-by-cell inspection reveals that (*wait, large*) strictly dominates (*wait, wait*) because of Eq. (5.4). Moreover, (*small, wait*) and (*wait, small*) will either be dominated by (*small, small*) if $\frac{1}{2}r - c > 0$ holds, or by (*wait, large*) otherwise. These strategies can be eliminated as any Nash equilibrium strategy profile does not include strictly dominated strategies.[3] The complete 5×5 game, then, can be reduced to a 2×2 matrix as shown in Fig. 5.4, containing the strategies (*small, small*) and (*wait, large*) for each terror organization.

[3]See Nash (1951) for a detailed analysis.

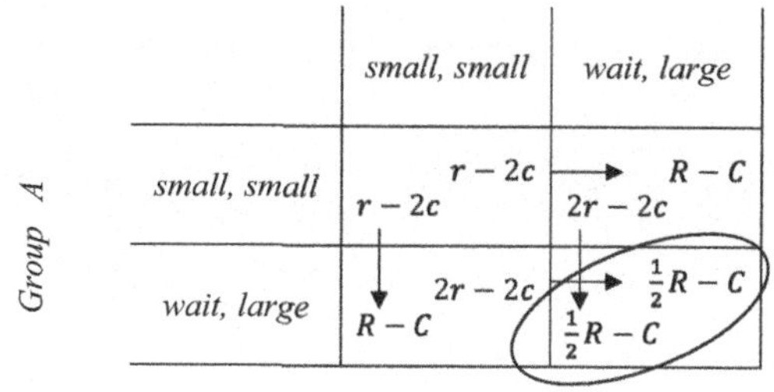

Fig. 5.5 Reduced game (case a)

Due to the inequalities (5.1) and (5.6), each group prefers to wait at the first stage and to carry out a large-scale attack at the subsequent stage, given the other organization plays (*small, small*).

Provided one group chooses (*wait, large*) the other faces

$$2r - 2c \gtrless \frac{1}{2}R - C \tag{5.9}$$

or, equivalently,

$$2\left(r - \frac{1}{4}R\right) \gtrless 2c - C. \tag{5.10}$$

Because of $2c < C$ by assumption, the right-hand side is always negative. However, which sign holds, is not evident, requiring a case differentiation: either the rewards of a large-scale attack are vastly superior to that of a small-scale incident or they are just superior. As Eq. (5.10) shows, the critical threshold turns out to be $4r \gtrless R$, i.e., the case $4r < R$ will be interpreted as being vastly superior.

Case (a)

For $2r - 2c < \frac{1}{2}R - C$, both groups prefer to wait at the first and conduct a large-scale attack at the second stage, so the unique Nash-equilibrium will be [*wait, large; wait, large*].

Referring to Eq. (5.10), the situation depicted in Fig. 5.5 occurs if, first, $4r < R$ holds and, second, the margin of rewards on the left-hand side is smaller than that of the costs on the right-hand side, which is negative due to $2c < C$. Then, (*wait, large*) dominates all other strategies and the outcome is Pareto-efficient. The result suggests that, in this model, terrorist groups have no incentive to engage in collusive behavior as there is no scenario, in which both groups are better off.

Case (b)

If $2r - 2c > \frac{1}{2}R - C$ holds, multiple Nash-equilibria exist, namely two off-diagonal pure-strategy Nash-equilibria [*small, small*; *wait, large*] and [*wait, large*; *small, small*], implying the existence of at least one mixed Nash-equilibrium.

Fig. 5.6 Reduced game (case b)

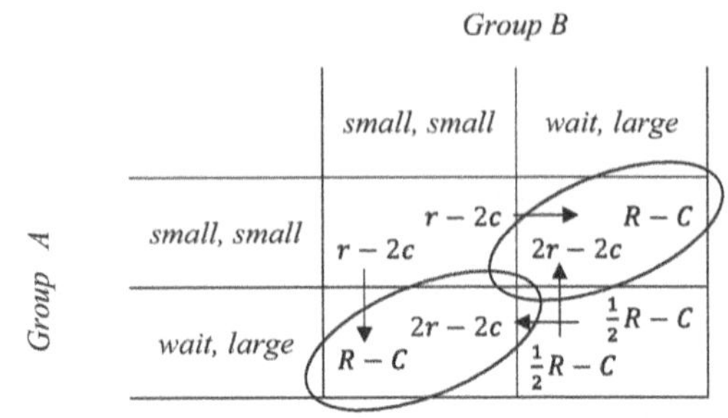

For $4r \geq R$, the inequality is certainly satisfied. However, even if the rewards associated with a large-scale attack are vastly superior to that of a small-scale incident, i.e., $4r < R$, the inequality may still hold if the margin of rewards is larger, meaning less negative, than the margin of costs (Fig. 5.6).

The solution to the game also consists of one equilibrium in mixed strategies. Mixing multiple pure strategies implies playing one action or another with certain probabilities (Nash 1951, p. 286). Here, in the only mixed-strategy equilibrium, each group mixes on two of five strategies, namely (*small*, *small*) and (*wait*, *large*), with weights $\left(0, 0, \frac{2r-2c-\left(\frac{1}{2}R-C\right)}{\frac{1}{2}R+r}, \frac{R-C-(r-2c)}{\frac{1}{2}R+r}, 0\right)$.[4] Such an equilibrium may explain why terrorism is often perceived to be random.

Depending on the proportionality of R and r, the quality of the two off-diagonal pure-strategy Nash-equilibria differs. Comparing the payoffs associated with [*small*, *small*; *wait*, *large*] and [*wait*, *large*; *small*, *small*] respectively, that is,

$$2r - 2c \gtrless R - C \tag{5.11}$$

or

$$2r - R \gtrless 2c - C \tag{5.12}$$

show that each group prefers the equilibrium, in which it plays (*small*, *small*) and the other chooses (*wait*, *large*), if $2r > R$ holds true.[5] On the other hand, if $2r < R$ is true, it is not evident, which equilibrium is preferred by each group because both sides are negative.

Assuming symmetry implies that the preferences of group A and group B are identical, meaning that both organizations prefer the same strategy, either (*small*, *small*) or (*wait*, *large*), but, therefore, favor different Nash-equilibria. In a competitive and dynamic environment, the groups then will find themselves in a race for either two small-scale attacks or a spectacular incident, each race bearing different implications for the effect of competition on terrorist group behavior. The group

[4]For a precise derivation, see Appendix A.

[5]Note that $2r > R$ does not violate (1) but now $2r - 2c > R - C$ holds due to $2c < C$.

capable of realizing the strategy of its favored equilibrium first may force the other to adapt and, thereby, can gain a higher payoff.

5.1.1 Why Large-Scale Attacks Occur At All

Under the conditions of case (b), suppose that each terror organization prefers to conduct two small-scale attacks while hoping the other plays (*wait*, *large*), so that

$$2r - 2c > R - C \tag{5.13}$$

holds.

Without the existence of other terrorist groups, the organization would simply conduct two small-scale attacks. However, due to rivalry a race for who can commit a small-scale attack first and thereby determine which equilibrium is played occurs. The group capable of conducting a small event first compels the other terrorist organization to play (*wait*, *large*) and receives the highest possible payoff. The loser of the race, that is, the slower one, although also preferring two small-scale attacks, will carry out a large-scale attack during stage two because of Eqs. (5.1) and (5.6).

The ability to commit an attack first is in a terrorist group's best interest because the possibility to set the stage for a slower player will provide the faster group with the highest possible payoff, provided the slower terrorist organization can react and adapt to the behavior of the first, i.e., each period can be played sequentially. Then a group can capitalize on a first-mover advantage.

However, this potential advantage can result in logistical failure. If both groups know that being the first to conduct a small-scale attack is advantageous, the probability of success may decrease as both groups try to conduct a small-scale attack as soon as possible and, thereby, increase their risk of failure, either because the groups are ill-prepared, or attackers become careless and attract attention as has been the case of the failed attacks on aircraft by al-Qaeda followers Umar Farouk Abdulmutallab and Richard Reid, known as the "underwear bomber" and the "shoe bomber," respectively (The Economist 2015).

Furthermore, in an environment of uncertainty,[6] at the extreme, both might commit a small-scale event at the same time or without observing the action of the other terror organization respectively, ending up with a worse outcome, $r - 2c$, for each player. The situation becomes even more "catastrophic" from terrorist groups' perspective if $\frac{1}{2}r - c < 0$ holds true, because then, both groups would have been better off if they do not carry out a second small-scale attack during period two because of $\frac{1}{2}r - c > r - 2c$.

[6]The representation of a game in normal form does not only imply that players act simultaneously but also that players cannot observe the actions of others.

To that effect, the scenario described is reminiscent of a chicken-situation:[7] a failure on the part of both sides to yield leads to an outcome that is disastrous to both. In versions of the chicken game, the disastrous outcome is usually associated with war or with the bankruptcy of rival firms. Here, in an understated form, the worst situation from an organization's perspective emerges when terrorist organizations use up their resources with little or no effect.

In order to obtain a higher payoff and to gain from a first-mover advantage, game theory provides the idea of strategic moves that change the rules of the original game by turning a simultaneous game into a sequential one and, thereby, changing the game to an actor's own advantage. These strategic moves are usually classified into commitment, threat, and promise[8] that serve the purpose to alter the actions of another player (Schelling 1960, pp. 122–123). However, it is in the nature of things that terrorist attacks rely on surprise, and groups keep their plans vague. Thus, strategic moves prove to be ineffective in the context of competing terrorist groups to force the rival to deter or compel a certain behavior.[9] The only way, in fact, to benefit from a potential advantage is to take the initiative, which, in turn, may result in attack failure.

The outbidding theory predicts an escalation of terrorist activity due to competitive behavior. In the notion of outbidding, a reduction of terrorist incidents is mainly incentivized due to a lack of violence acceptance among the group of supporters (Downs 1957; Chenoweth 2010), so rival terrorist groups tend to reduce their terrorist behavior in order to gather support. Alternatively, reduced terrorist activity is explained by increased counterterrorism efforts if groups strategically complement each other, while groups that are substitutes tend to increase their activities (Siqueira 2005).

The findings of the model indicate that competition and the alleged first-mover advantage relating to it can explain why some terrorist attack attempts fail. If time pressure makes logistical failure more likely due to a lack of precision, competition between groups can lead to less terrorism. Not exogenous factors, e.g., a shift in attitudes of the followership or state responses to terrorism, but rivalry itself can

[7]In its original version, two youngsters are driving toward each other at high speed on a road. Each player has the option to swerve or to drive straight on. If one swerves and the other does not, the player, who swerves, loses and is the chicken, while the other is the winner. If both swerve it is a tie and if none swerves the game ends in mutual destruction (Rapoport and Chammah 1966). Of course, the present game is not a chicken-type game for two reasons. First, the game between two terrorist organizations technically consists of five strategies, and the analogy to the chicken game is found for the reduced form. Second, the original version of chicken usually depicts a situation of two opponents situated in direct confrontation, which is not the case here. Nevertheless, the analysis exhibits certain parallels and contains some interesting features.

[8]On the theory of strategic moves, see Schelling (1960).

[9]This is especially true for conditional moves. In this context, even a commitment, an unconditional move, seems to be unreasonable since this would mean that one terrorist organization credibly and irreversibly declares to conduct two small-scale attacks instead of one large attack. Although terrorist groups pronounce their purpose to attack—a kind of commitment—note that the question here is not on attacking or not attacking, but on when and to what extent.

reduce the number of incidents. Competition, and more precisely, the existence of a first-mover advantage between substitutes, can have the opposite effect on terrorist activity than suggested by defenders of the outbidding theory.

Furthermore, given $2r - 2c > R - C$ and the emergence of a race for which group will carry out a small-scale attack first, competition, then, will lead to a situation, in which a large-scale incident will occur at all. Without rivalry merely small-scale attacks are carried out due to the preferences. In the case of competition, however, the slower group will shift from playing (*small, small*) to (*wait, large*), that is, the loser will carry out a large-scale attack as a result of competition, while the race's winner does not lose anything due to competition, provided the probability of success does not change due to rivalry. Hence, competition can explain the occurrence of large-scale attacks.

5.1.2 A Not So Obvious Dominant Strategy

Provided the conditions of case (b) are still valid, suppose now that

$$2r - 2c < R - C \tag{5.14}$$

or

$$r - c < \frac{1}{2}(R - C) \tag{5.15}$$

respectively hold true, so that each terror organization favors a Nash-equilibrium, in which it conducts a large-scale attack while the other plays (*small, small*). Then, condition (5.15) gives rise to a race for which group can conduct a large-scale incident first. However, carrying out a spectacular event is only possible during the second period by assumption. Although the game is formally modeled as a two-period game, a rigid division of periods concerning the end of stage one and the beginning of stage two may be too demanding. Rather, suppose that each terrorist organization begins to plan and prepare a spectacular event. Then, the preparation time is equivalent to the first stage and the second stage starts with a large-scale attack's implementation by one of the two.

The group incapable of carrying out a large-scale attack first, i.e., the slower one, then either can commit a large-scale attack as well, thereby diminishing the winner's payoff from $R - C$ to $\frac{1}{2}R - C$, or can carry out a small-scale attack during period two.

However, if the loser of the race prefers (*wait, small*) instead of (*wait, large*) at stage two, that is, if

$$r - c > \frac{1}{2}R - C \tag{5.16}$$

is assumed to hold, the terror organization would have been better off by carrying out two small-scale attacks from the very beginning and can obtain a higher payoff by not engaging in the race for a large-scale attack.

Furthermore, the decision on whether to conduct an additional spectacular event or to play (*wait, small*), when being the slower group at stage two, is affected by the costs already incurred for the preparation of a large-scale attack during the first period, which may represent sunk costs, when carrying out a small-scale incident at the second stage.

From Eqs. (5.15) and (5.16) follows that

$$r - c \in \left(\frac{1}{2}R - C, \frac{1}{2}(R - C)\right). \tag{5.17}$$

If a terror organization prepares a large-scale attack and then switches to a small-scale attack during period two, the associated payoff $r - c$ is reduced by the amount of the costs, which accrue from the preparation of a large-scale attack during period one. The interval length. The interval length of $\frac{1}{2}C$ indicates that these costs have to be smaller than $\frac{1}{2}C$ in order that playing small at the second stage will be considered, i.e.,

$$FC < \frac{1}{2}C \tag{5.18}$$

must hold true.

For $FC > \frac{1}{2}C$, the slower group will not switch to a small-scale attack at stage two but will commit an additional spectacular event. If both groups have no idea what the other will do or if the other's actions are not observable, then the solution to the game will be the mixed-strategy equilibrium derived in Sect. 5.1.1.

If $FC < \frac{1}{2}C$ holds true, the losing group participating in the race for a large-scale attack would be willing to abandon a large-scale attack and to conduct a small-scale attack at stage two. However, as noted an organization could improve its payoff by not participating in the race but committing two small-scale attacks from the beginning. The extensive form of the game depicted in Fig. 5.7 illustrates the decision-making problem under the conditions described.

For the sake of clarity only the subgame, if both decide to wait, which is interpreted as preparing a large-scale attack at stage one, is presented in detail for period two. If one of the two organizations—or even both—commits a small-scale attack during the first period, the outcomes do not differ from the already known ones (see Fig. 5.4). However, if both groups choose to participate in the race for a large-scale attack, each group can win—or lose respectively—with a probability of one-half. Thus, the decision to participate in the race for a spectacular event and to risk losing depends on the expected payoff relating to a large-scale attack's outcome,

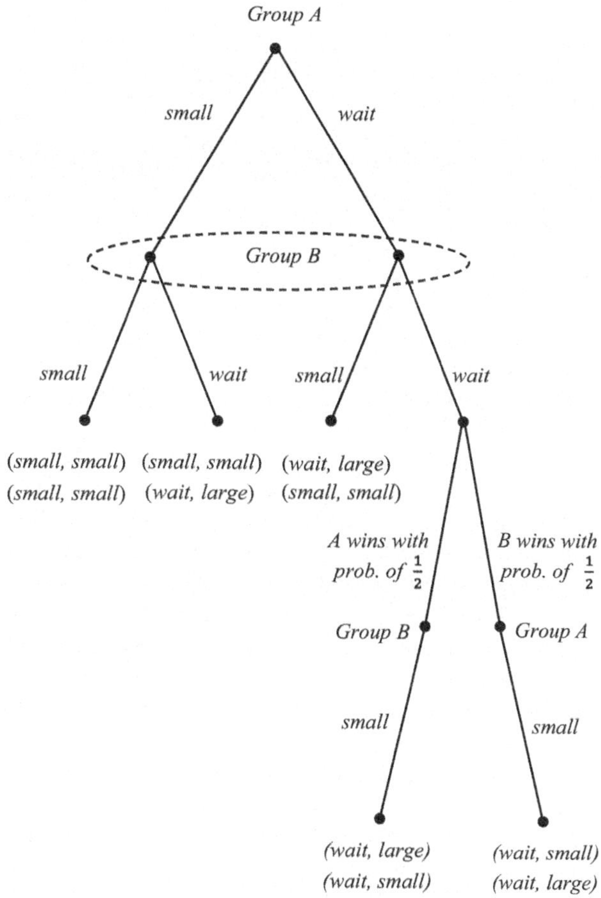

Fig. 5.7 Extensive form

when winning the race, and the outcome associated with playing (*wait*, *small*), when losing, that is,

$$\begin{aligned} EV &= \frac{1}{2}(\textit{wait}, \textit{large}) + \frac{1}{2}(\textit{wait}, \textit{small}) \\ &= \frac{1}{2}(R - C) + \frac{1}{2}(r - c - FC). \end{aligned} \tag{5.19}$$

If and only if

$$\frac{1}{2}(R - C) + \frac{1}{2}(r - c - FC) > 2r - 2c \tag{5.20}$$

or

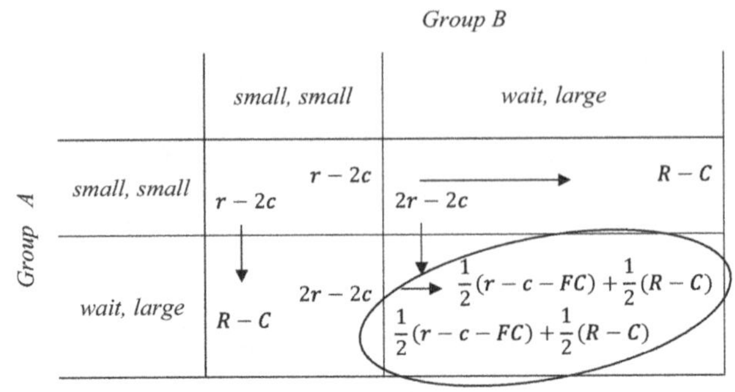

Fig. 5.8 Participating in a race for large-scale attacks. Note: Here, the strategy (*wait, large*) is to be understood in the sense of participating in the race for a large-scale attack. However, this may also entail committing a small-scale attack at stage two

$$R - C - 3(r - c) > FC \tag{5.21}$$

hold true, the expected value from participating in the race is larger than the payoff from conducting two small-scale attacks.

If the investments during the first period are sufficiently small, from each group's perspective waiting during period one, meaning participating in a large-scale attack race and preparing the event, and trying to capitalize on being first to conduct a large-scale attack at stage two is always better, independent from the other group's choice for period one (Fig. 5.8).[10]

Is it conceivable to imagine that the fixed costs are sufficiently small? Usually, the major part—if not all—costs that are irreversible can be assumed to incur shortly before an attack is conducted, or even during the attack. For example, a vehicle is rented (or stolen) on the day of the attack, or a perpetrator is sent to the location of an attack shortly before conducting an attack in order to minimize the risk of detection.

The inequality certainly is not satisfied, when comparing 9/11 and car bombings in Raqqa, Kabul, or Mosul. However, the attacks against critical infrastructures, such as those against the London transportation system in 2005, may be regarded as a large-scale attack, whereas the vehicle-ramming attacks in Nice, Berlin, or Graz, then, may represent small-scale attacks. To that effect, it is plausible to assume that the cost incurred for the preparation of a large-scale attack during period one, that may be sunk, when carrying out a small-scale attack as a second-mover at stage two instead, are sufficiently small or even negligible due to the fact that these costs will accrue at the second stage of the game. Thus, if groups compete for committing large-scale attacks, the findings suggest that each group has a dominant strategy for participating in the race, despite the risk to lose—a scenario that is not directly evident, when considering the initial situation of case (b).

[10]Note that the term "dominant strategy" here is avoided because playing *wait* in period one does not describe a strategy of the game as already explained in Sect. 5.1.

Fig. 5.9 Multiple Nash-equilibria for $FC < \frac{1}{2}C$

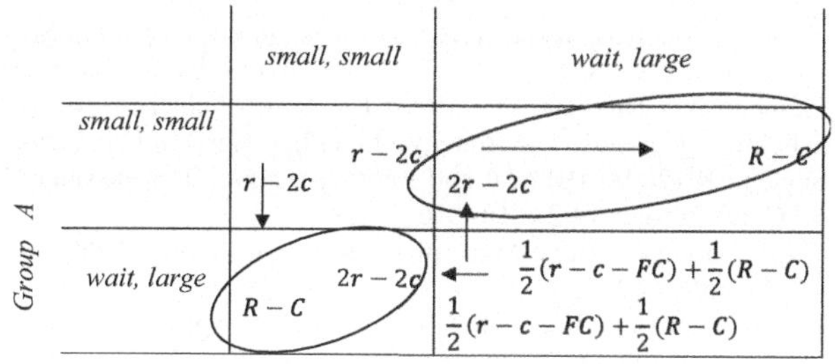

For $R - C - 3(r - c) < FC$, the game would result in multiple Nash-equilibria as illustrated in Fig. 5.9 and the terror organizations will play their mixed strategies with weights $\left(0, 0, \frac{3(r-c)-(R-C)+FC}{r+c+R-C+FC}, \frac{2(R-C)-2(r-2c)}{r+c+R-C+FC}, 0\right)$.[11]

As has been the case with favoring two small-scale attacks, the parameter constellation will lead to a race for carrying out a spectacular event and, if believing that one of two organizations can capitalize on being first, may decrease the probability of success if both groups try to conduct a large-scale attack as soon as possible.

Apart from the previously discussed effects of competition on terrorist group behavior, what makes this case so special is the wide-held belief that major terrorist attacks increase the risk of further attacks, and terrorist incidents occur in clusters (Jenkins et al. 2016). If there is one attack, another will follow soon, and other groups try to jump on the bandwagon of terror (Bloom 2004). The game-theoretic consideration, however, suggests that other groups are not inspired by a spectacular event, but a follow-up action is the result of sequential play triggered by the winner of the race.

References

Besenyo J (2017) Low-cost attacks, unnoticeable plots? Overview on the economical character of current terrorism. Strateg Impact 63(1):83–100

Bloom MM (2004) Palestinian suicide bombing: Public support, market share, and outbidding. Political Science Quarterly 119(1):61–88

Chenoweth E (2010) Democratic competition and terrorist activity. J Polit 72(1):16–30

Conrad J, Greene K (2015) Competition, differentiation, and the severity of terrorist attacks. J Polit 77(2):546–561

Downs A (1957) An economic theory of political action in a democracy. J Polit Econ 65 (2):135–150

Jenkins BM, Willis HH, Han B (2016) Do significant terrorist attacks increase the risk of further attacks? Initial observations from a statistical analysis of terrorist attacks in the United States and Europe from 1970 to 2013. RAND Corporation, Santa Monica, CA

[11]See Appendix B for a precise derivation.

Kremer M (1993) The O-ring theory of economic development. Q J Econ 108(3):551–575
Nash J (1951) Non-cooperative games. Ann Math 54(2):286–295
National Commission on Terrorist Attacks upon the United States (2004) The 9/11 commission report. Accessed 14 Aug 2018. http://govinfo.library.unt.edu/911/report/911Report.pdf
Rapoport A, Chammah AM (1966) The game of chicken. Am Behav Sci 10(3):10–28
Schelling TC (1960) The strategy of conflict. Harvard University Press, Cambridge
Siqueira K (2005) Political and militant wings within dissident movements and organizations. J Confl Resolut 49(2):218–236
The Economist (2015) Aviation security – no more of the same please. The Economist 2015, November 14
United States Department of Defense (2011) Background briefing with senior intelligence official at the pentagon on intelligence aspects of the U.S. Operation Involving Osama Bin Laden. Accessed 14 Oct 2018. http://archive.defense.gov/transcripts/transcript.aspx?transcriptid=4820
Windrem R (2015) Terror on a shoestring: Paris attacks likely cost $10,000 or less. Accessed 14 Nov 2018. https://www.nbcnews.com/storyline/paris-terror-attacks/terror-shoestring-paris-attacks-likely-cost-10-000-or-less-n465711

Chapter 6
Al-Qaeda and *Daesh*: The Rise of the Islamic State

Abstract Terrorist organizations are often assumed to be homogenous. Not only do groups claim to represent the same population and, therefore, compete for the same sponsorship, but terrorists also follow the same objectives. This homogeneity indicates that these groups similarly value benefits and costs and that payoffs are symmetrical. Although this may apply to past scenarios, e.g., Palestinian, Northern Ireland, and other, mainly secular-driven terrorist incidents, recent developments among jihadi-related groups have proven to be different. Despite their jihadist ideologies and their ultimate desire to establish a caliphate, *al-Qaeda* and *Daesh* are far from being similar. *Daesh* attracted international attention for its involvement in the full-scale civil war in Syria, but it did not simply appear in 2014 to replace *al-Qaeda*, as the Western media often suggests. This group already had strongholds in Syria, e.g., Raqqa, and precursors that were part of the *al-Qaeda* network can be traced back more than a decade before *Daesh*'s emergence and its subsequent global recognition. The organization used means that were not tolerated by *al-Qaeda*, leading *al-Qaeda* to cut ties with it. This renunciation indicates that treating *al-Qaeda* and *Daesh* as equal does not capture the full scope of these movements' relationship, even though the groups may be perceived as substitutes for one another.

Terrorist organizations are often assumed to be homogenous. Not only do groups claim to represent the same population and, therefore, compete for the same sponsorship, but terrorists also follow the same objectives. This homogeneity indicates that these groups similarly value benefits and costs and that payoffs are symmetrical. Although this may apply to past scenarios, e.g., Palestinian, Northern Ireland, and other, mainly secular-driven terrorist incidents, recent developments among jihadi-related groups have proven to be different. Despite their jihadist ideologies and their ultimate desire to establish a caliphate, *al-Qaeda* and *Daesh* are far from being similar. *Daesh* attracted international attention for its involvement in the full-scale civil war in Syria, but it did not simply appear in 2014 to replace *al-Qaeda*, as the Western media often suggests. This group already had strongholds in Syria, e.g., Raqqa, and precursors that were part of the *al-Qaeda* network can be traced back more than a decade before *Daesh*'s emergence and its subsequent global recognition. The organization used means that were not tolerated by *al-Qaeda*, leading *al-Qaeda*

© The Author(s), under exclusive license to Springer Nature Switzerland AG 2020
N. Ismael, *Strategic Interaction Between Islamist Terror Groups*, SpringerBriefs in Economics, https://doi.org/10.1007/978-3-030-51307-8_6

to cut ties with it. This renunciation indicates that treating *al-Qaeda* and *Daesh* as equal does not capture the full scope of these movements' relationship, even though the groups may be perceived as substitutes for one another.

This chapter seeks to highlight the rivalry between the two movements and the impact of this on their activities. Section 6.1 describes the genesis of *al-Qaeda*, its former official offshoot *Jabhat Fateh al-Sham*, and *Daesh* and provides insight into their relationship. In addition to their history, the leaders' different socioeconomic backgrounds and other factors help explain the groups' different approaches in the fight for dominance. Furthermore, their different objectives and methods are used to transfer and apply the model of competition derived in Chap. 5 to the situation of *Jabhat Fateh al-Sham* and *Daesh* in Sect. 6.2 and *al-Qaeda* and *Daesh* in Sect. 6.3 as both case studies are considered separately.

6.1 Origins and *Raisons d'être*

The Palestinian ideologue and mentor of Osama bin Laden, Abdullah Yusuf Azzam, issued a fatwa (an authoritative legal opinion or interpretation) named the "Defense of the Muslim Lands," when the Soviet Union invaded Afghanistan in 1979. In this fatwa, he formulated the imperative of liberating the holy lands occupied by foreign powers and the personal obligation of all Muslims to kill the occupiers. The 10-year occupation, which lasted until 1989, induced Muslims to fight against a major opponent and facilitated the emergence of jihadism (Yusufzai 2001).

Inspired by Azzam's word and his engagement in the fight against the Soviets, Osama bin Laden followed the call. With the financial help of bin Laden, Azzam managed to mobilize and organize resistance against the Soviets (Yusufzai 2001) and with his pamphlet, Azzam laid the foundation for the jihadism al-Qaeda became known for.

The first Gulf War (1990–1991) spurred on *al-Qaeda*'s emergence. Following the Iraqi invasion of Kuwait under Saddam Hussein, the deployment of more than half a million troops by the United States and its allies in Saudi Arabia was condemned by bin Laden, who perceived this as the presence of "infidel" troops in the birthplace of Islam. To defend Saudi Arabia from further aggression by Hussein, bin Laden planned to recruit Arab veterans, who had fought in Afghanistan against the Soviets. Saudi Arabia declined his proposal, however, and in addition to the deployment, the refusal by the Saudi Royal Family seeded animosity against the United States and caused bin Laden to flee and settle in Sudan (Brownstein and Wright 2001).

In 1996, under pressure from Americans and Saudis, Sudanese authorities forced bin Laden out of the country, and he relocated to Afghanistan. Here, he declared war against the United States and *al-Qaeda* was born. Following the formation of *al-Qaeda*, bin Laden established a formal organization that comprised jihadists from Saudi Arabia, Egypt, and North Africa (Brownstein and Wright 2001).

Al-Qaeda was held responsible for the attack on the World Trade Center in 1993, the bombings at United States' embassies in Tanzania and Kenia in 1998, and the

2000 bombing of the *USS Cole*. Bin Laden's' aggression against the United States peaked in the attacks on the World Trade Center and the Pentagon in 2001. Around the same time, Jordan Abu Musab al-Zarqawi (originally Ahmad Fadhil Nazzal al-Khalaylah) formed *Jama'at al-Tawhid Wahl-Jihad*, an initially negligible Sunni militant group (Zelin 2014).

During his time in Afghanistan, bin Laden was worshipped among the Afghan Arabs and gained increasing leverage, not only due to the attacks in and against the United States but also because of his wealth and the unsuccessful attempts of other local jihadist groups in the early 1990s (Zelin 2014).

Bin Laden and al-Zarqawi first met in 1999 in Afghanistan. The latter wished to operate a training camp in Herat, Afghanistan, with followers, who had been released because of Jordanian prison amnesty earlier in the year and were faithful to al-Zarqawi. To create his camp, al-Zarqawi sought help, and bin Laden provided him with financial assistance (Whitlock 2004).

It soon became apparent, however, that there were tensions between bin Laden and al-Zarqawi. Their relationship was characterized by significant friction and distrust, not least because of their different socioeconomic backgrounds. It is a well-known fact that Osama bin Laden and his close followers were raised upper-middle-class families and had studied at university, whereas al-Zarqawi and his entourage hailed from poorer, less educated backgrounds. Saltman and Winter (2014, p. 27) further note that al-Zarqawi had been a "*petty criminal, who [appeared] to have struggled with alcoholism in his youth.*" Al-Zarqawi's criminal past and his extreme views on accusing another Muslim of apostasy to justify his killing laid the foundation of discord between bin Laden and himself (Saltman and Winter 2014).

Around the time of the 9/11 attacks, al-Zarqawi was suspected to be in Iran, where he met with a Jordan ally and ordered him to set up a cell in Germany to strike Jewish targets there. Following the 9/11 attacks, US forces invaded Afghanistan and weakened *al-Qaeda* by capturing and killing its core members. al-Zarqawi left Iran, went back to Afghanistan, and joined the ranks of *al-Qaeda* and the Taliban (Whitlock 2004).

It is suspected that al-Zarqawi left Afghanistan because he was injured and changed its whereabouts between Iran, Syria, and the Sunni Triangle, where he acquired new jihadist contacts. It is unclear, when al-Zarqawi moved to Iraq, but within a short time after the United States' decision to cast out Saddam Hussein, the invasion of Iraq, and the deployment of tens of thousands of troops to create a new ally in Baghdad, he became known for his brutal beheadings and suicide bombing campaigns against both Shiites and Sunni civilians. These "successes" led to an increase of (foreign) fighters joining his cause, leading to an increased need for resources (Rabasa et al. 2006).

Due to these developments, al-Zarqawi swore a religious oath (*baya*) to the *al-Qaeda* leader. This alleged obsequiousness benefitted both al-Zarqawi and bin Laden as despite hiding from the United States, bin Laden wanted to remain important and marshal an Iraqi holy war. al-Zarqawi wanted access to the resources he needed to manage the increase in supporters. After renaming al-Zarqawi's movement *al-Qaeda in the Land of Two Rivers*, better known as *al-Qaeda in Iraq*, bin Laden was able to establish an *al-Qaeda* offshoot in Iraq (Zelin 2014).

Al-Zarqawi's integration into the *al-Qaeda* network in 2004 was, however, no more than a partnership of convenience. *Al-Qaeda* propagated a unified Islamic front against the West, whereas *Al-Qaeda in Iraq* prioritized the purge of the Islamic community. This was demonstrated by the fact that a*l-Qaeda in Iraq* engaged in brutal denominational killings, much to the dismay of its parent organization. Ayman al-Zawahiri, at that time bin Laden's second in command, warned al-Zarqawi that attacks by *al-Qaeda in Iraq* on Shiite civilians and other Muslims "*won't be acceptable to the Muslim populace*" (al-Zawahiri 2005, p. 8).

Al-Zarqawi's belief that Shiites and anyone else he and his movement imagined embodying apostate Muslims deserved death caused an ideological divide between al-Zarqawi and bin Laden. The former's attitude created tension not only with his parent organization but also with his mentor and the ideological leader of *al-Qaeda in Iraq*, Sheikh Abu Muhammad al-Maqdisi, who urged al-Zarqawi to refrain from shortsighted fighting strategies and instead focus on consolidating gains (Wagemakers 2011). Nevertheless, al-Zarqawi pursued his purges.

In 2005, the discontent surrounding his actions and ongoing brutality led to serious alerts by al-Zawahiri and the *al-Qaeda* ideologue Sheikh Atiyat Allah Abd al-Rahman al-Libi, who exhorted al-Zarqawi to soften his actions and enforcement of Sharia law in order to not endanger the overall goal of global jihadism (al-Zawahiri 2005).

Al-Qaeda in Iraq under al-Zarqawi became one of *al-Qaeda*'s most powerful branches, and the focus began shifting from the global parent organization to its affiliate. Even al-Zarqawi's death as the result of a United States air strike in June 2006 did not immediately affect *al-Qaeda in Iraq*'s success or its ongoing popularity. The death of al-Zarqawi canceled his oath to bin Laden, but *al-Qaeda* and *al-Qaeda in Iraq* continued cooperating. At the end of 2006, *al-Qaeda in Iraq* rebranded itself as the *Islamic State of Iraq*, and Abu Omar al-Baghdadi became its new leader (Zelin 2014).

Although al-Zarqawi had fervent followers, his successors could not preserve his heritage, and they lost major support in Iraq. The *Islamic State of Iraq*'s mode of governance was fateful, and the warnings of al-Libi and al-Zawahiri turned out to be true: the narrow perspective and harsh enforcement of Sharia law induced a backlash by residents and other Sunni Iraqi insurgent groups and led to the prospering of the so-called *awakening* movement in the form of a Sunni militia group (Fishman 2009).

During "the surge"[1] in 2007, many Iraqi Sunni fighters and former insurgents sided with the Americans and forced the *Islamic State in Iraq* to retreat and held it at bay. Following the death of Abu Omar al-Baghdadi in 2010, he was replaced by Abu Bakr al-Baghdadi, an Islamic scholar, who had spent 10 months in captivity in the United States before being released as a potential low-level threat (Zelin 2014).

[1]The surge refers to the reinforcement in the number of American troops and a change in strategy for the use of forces in Iraq (Crider 2009).

There is reason to believe that *al-Qaeda* tried to capitalize on the weakening of the *Islamic State in Iraq*, but that it was not necessarily successful because *al-Qaeda* still backed the group publicly, although the decrease of the *Islamic State in Iraq*'s popularity confirmed al-Libi's and al-Zawahiri's position. In a public release, al-Zawahiri proclaimed that cooperating with the mujahedin in Iraq (and by association supporting the *Islamic State of Iraq*) was an important obligation (al-Zawahiri 2008, p. 19).

The setback of the *Islamic State in Iraq* led to a significant reduction in violent attacks across Iraq and allowed for the eventual withdrawal of the bulk of American forces. In preparation for departure, the Americans installed a Shia Government, which suppressed Sunni minorities at a very early stage, e.g., the previously mentioned *awakening* movement, which sided with the United States. The American-appointed government, therefore, harmed the initial success of the mission to combat the *Islamic State of Iraq* and gave the movement scope for effecting a revival.

Only a few months after bin Laden's death in 2011, an *Islamic State in Iraq* spokesman officially accepted the announced appointment of al-Zawahiri as *al-Qaeda*'s new leader (al-Adnani 2011, p. 5).

The *Islamic State in Iraq* spent several years reforming. This process was promoted by the chaos caused by the uprisings in neighboring Syria and the political failures of the Iraqi Government (and of course the United States' withdrawal). It started its comeback in 2011, when al-Baghdadi delegated operatives to Syria to establish a new jihadist organization and to expand al-Zarqawi's statehood project. Among the delegated operatives was Abu Muhammad al-Julani, the later leader of *Jabhat-al-Nusra*, a group that arose from the *Islamic State of Iraq*.

Jabhat-al-Nusra was officially announced at the beginning of 2012 after sufficient jihadist fighters moved from Iraq to Syria during the *Islamic State of Iraq*'s expansion and gained sufficient support. In the shortest time possible, *Jabhat-al-Nusra* became one of the best fighting forces under Julani's guidance, and the locals viewed its members as fair arbiters, when addressing corruption and the provision of social services (Mortada 2014).

In 2013, al-Baghdadi tried to unite *Jabhat-al-Nusra* and the *Islamic State of Iraq* and renamed it *Islamic State of Iraq and al-Sham.* An official declaration by al-Baghdadi that he was expanding the movement to Syria caused antagonism with *al-Qaeda* and *Daesh* as this course of action had not been agreed upon by *al-Qaeda*'s leadership (al-Baghdadi 2013). Al-Baghdadi and al-Julani disagreed mainly on strategy, which caused al-Julani to turn pledge allegiance to al-Zawahiri and, by association, *al-Qaeda* (al-Julani 2013).

Al-Zawahiri prompted al-Baghdadi to cede Syria to *Jabhat-al-Nusra* and return to Iraq. According to McCants (2013), al-Baghdadi stated that *Daesh* would not retreat from Syria. As a result, in 2013, *Jabhat-al-Nusra* formally split from al-Baghdadi's group and began competing militarily for the same areas in Syria and Lebanon's Qalamoun mountains (McCants 2013).

Daesh occupied the Syrian provincial capital of Raqqa and continued to encourage its statehood project at the start of 2014. After an uprising against *Daesh* by mainstream Syrian rebels due to the movement's general predatory approach of taking territory and resources from other insurgencies (Zelin 2014), *al-Qaeda*'s general command released a statement in February 2014, in which *al-Qaeda* cut ties with *Daesh*, stating that it "*is not a branch of the Qaedat al-Jihad group, we have no organizational relationship with it, and the group [Al-Qaeda] is not responsible for its actions*" (al-Qaeda's General Command 2014). Only a few months later, *Daesh* proclaimed a caliphate with its own government and bureaucracy, with institutions enforcing its narrow interpretations of Sharia law.

The main disagreements between *al-Qaeda* and *Daesh* have long been about methodology and authority. Although the predecessor of *Daesh* pursued a policy of détente, *Daesh* believes that recent *al-Qaeda* activities have deviated from bin Laden's path and views al-Zawahiri as an illegitimate authority (al-Adnani 2014). From *al-Qaeda*'s perspective, al-Baghdadi and *Daesh* violated a religious oath. *Daesh* represents a deviant group that flouts al-Zawahiri's order to carry out jihad in its designated location of Iraq (al-Zawahiri 2014).

At the end of 2016 and in early 2017, *al-Qaeda* officially comprised five formal affiliates. It is a network of functional branches and informal allies in the Middle East, Asia, and Africa (Soufan Group Report 2017). Its Syrian branch, *Jabhat-al-Nusra*, was thought to have at least 5000 fighters by mid-2014 and according to the Pentagon, this number had increased to 10,000 by the end of 2016. *Jabhat-al-Nusra* attracted more fighters than any other Syrian insurgency except *Daesh* (Soufan Group Report 2017).

In mid-2016, *Jabhat-al-Nusra* intimated that it would not keep up with other groups outside Syria and rebranded itself as *Jabhat Fateh al-Sham*. Officially cutting ties with *al-Qaeda* enabled the organization to deny any links, when cooperating or seeking an eventual alliance with groups that had opposed its affiliation to *al-Qaeda*. Interestingly, the former parent organization endorsed the segregation and, thereby, supports the assumption of an informal lasting relationship (Hassan and Barabandi 2016).

In recent years, the international community's focus has been on *Daesh*. However, *al-Qaeda* represents the pioneer of global jihadism, and it is attempting to retrieve its authority. Although *al-Qaeda*'s main goal of reforming society and governing it under a strict interpretation of Sharia law does not differ from the goal of *Daesh*, the two organizations vary in methodology and timeline. What drove fighters to follow bin Laden in the late twentieth century certainly is different from what motivated fighters to join *Daesh*.

Although *Daesh* originated from *al-Qaeda*, its development and autonomy came from several conflicts with its parent organization. The fundamental differences are rooted in the background of the groups' leaders and their attitude towards conducting Jihad.

The growth of *al-Qaeda* spawned various local franchises in the mid-2000s due to the success of the 9/11 attacks. The group backed local plots and insurgencies in the Arab world to supplement its efforts against Western targets.

Daesh's primary goal is capturing and directly governing territory, and it attempted public outreach by engaging in mass killings and beheadings (Dabiq 2014, p. 38). Regionally, *Daesh* relies on projecting ruthless strength to win over potential followers and criticizing other jihad groups for not prioritizing territorial governance (Dabiq 2014, p. 39). According to documents recovered from *al-Qaeda in Iraq* in 2009, *Daesh* intentionally derived revenue locally in order to avoid foreign dependence and direction (Johnston et al. 2016, pp. 8–9).

On the international stage, *Daesh* has conducted incidents at public gatherings, including a theater and outdoor café in Paris in late 2015 and Brussels airport in early 2016. Its social media and publications have repeatedly appealed for lone-wolf attacks. By the end of 2016, however, *Daesh* had lost major parts of its territory due to disparate forces in Iraq and Syria and daily airstrikes by a United States-led coalition. Although seeking territory has been the main concern for *Daesh*, it has built an external operations capability and is likely to endure over time.

In contrast, *al-Qaeda* seeks to establish a global jihad and views the United States and the West as greater enemies. This principle is as true today as it was 20 years ago. *The General Guidelines for Jihad* issued by al-Zawahiri confirm that the "*focus should be maintained on constantly weakening the head of international disbelief (America) until it bleeds to death both militarily and financially*" (al-Zawahiri 2013, p. 3).

While *Daesh* has attracted attention during the last few years, *al-Qaeda* has had the chance to recover and capitalize on *Daesh*'s setbacks quietly.

6.2 Case Study: *Jabhat Fateh al-Sham* Versus *Daesh*

The previous section illustrated that *al-Qaeda* and *Daesh* pursue different organizational goals. Although both movements strive for global jihad, they vary in their objective functions. *Daesh* seeks to gain territory and local influence by subjugating the local population through ruthless behavior. In only a few months, *Daesh* seized territory and declared a caliphate. Contrarily, *al-Qaeda* has attempted to achieve tolerance for its cause, and to build alliances for a united jihad, despite its achievements having been less visible since 2011. With its many offshoots, *al-Qaeda* has local representatives and allies though. One branch is *Jabhat Fateh al-Sham* (originally emerged as *Jabhat al-Nusra* or *Nusra-Front*), a group, which operates in Syria and Iraq like *Daesh*.

Jabhat Fateh al-Sham is said to be one of the most powerful rebel groups in Syria and had up to an estimated number of 10.000 fighters by the end of 2016. During the initial stages of the Syrian civil war, *Jabhat Fateh al-Sham* claimed responsibility for 57 out of 70 suicide attacks (Roggio 2013). The *al-Qaeda* offshoot has managed to gain support from Syrians and attracted recruits by continuing to fight the Assad regime. However, it also established sharia courts in the territory, in which it operates.

According to al-Zawahiri, *Jabhat Fateh al-Sham* was *al-Qaeda*'s best chance of acquiring long-lasting territorial control in Syria and establishing a "safe base," from which to launch attacks on the West (al-Zawahiri 2013). However, *Jabhat Fateh al-Sham* realized that the *al-Qaeda* brand is toxic, which induced the group to

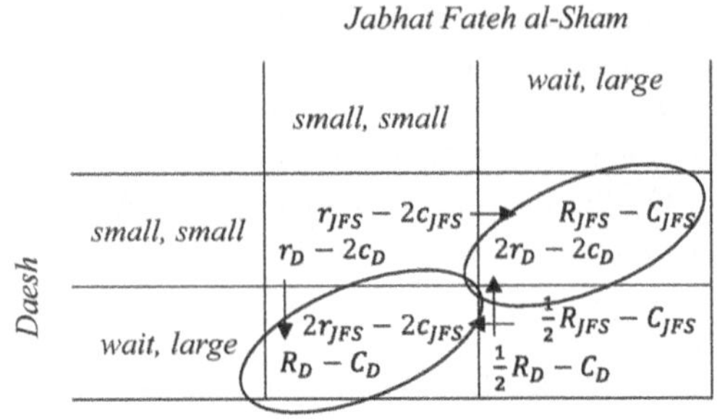

Fig. 6.1 *Jabhat Fateh Al-Sham* Versus *Daesh*

renounce officially. Nevertheless, the ties can be assumed to be very strong, so that *al-Qaeda* still has a branch in Syria.

Due to their local alignment, it is reasonable to suppose that *Jabhat Fateh al-Sham* and *Daesh* can be considered as relatively homogeneous concerning their preferences as both vie for local supremacy. The model, thus, can easily be applied to the rivalry between both terror organizations.

Still assuming $R_i - C_i > r_i - c_i$ with $i = D, JFS$, the assumption of local alignment implies

$$2r_i - 2c_i > R_i - C_i, \tag{6.1}$$

leading to a situation as depicted in Fig. 6.1.

Based on the assumptions, competition between *Daesh* and *Jabhat Fateh al-Sham* will lead to a situation, in which both groups participate in a race for two small-scale attacks. The organization, which is capable of committing a small-scale first at stage one, forces the other to carry out a large-scale attack during the second period if the game is interpreted sequentially. If each group has no clue, the groups are expected to play their mixed strategies.

Although the setbacks of *Daesh* are mainly driven by the efforts of different resistant forces in Iraq and Syria, the model and the corresponding case study provide an additional explanation for *Daesh*'s recent realignment to Western targets and attacks in Europe, particularly the multipronged incidents in Paris and Brussels. Apart from the lost grounds and setbacks of *Daesh*, the rivalry between *Daesh* and other terror organizations with similar preferences may have forced *Daesh* to commit a large-scale attack, which would imply that *Daesh* has lost the race, when interpreting "small-scale" as local and "large-scale" as global. This interpretation is supported by the fact that *Jabhat Fateh al-Sham* did not commit attacks on the global arena yet, so that—in the context of the model—it is conceivable that *Jabhat Fateh al-Sham* may have won the race.

Although *Daesh* is still trying to establish a local caliphate, competitive pressures, thus, can explain *Daesh*'s shift from the local to the global arena, although *Daesh* is still trying to establish a local caliphate.

6.3 Case Study: Towards a Model for *al-Qaeda* and *Daesh*

Although *al-Qaeda* has built on local allies in recent years, it remains the global jihadist movement that has proven to be able to threaten the West dramatically. It has the potential to be a more significant threat than *Daesh* in the long run. Not least a statement by al-Zawahiri revealed that *al-Qaeda* seeks for safe havens in order to launch attacks in the United States (al-Zawahiri 2013).

If it is true that *al-Qaeda* focuses on building strength across multiple countries and views the United States and the West as greater enemies than, for example, having little tolerance for Shiites and other minorities, i.e., being less exclusionary, *al-Qaeda* can be expected to address a major proportion within the extremist community than *Daesh*, so that $R_{AQ} > R_D$ is assumed to hold, demonstrating the intention of global alignment.

Conversely, *Daesh*'s efforts and successes to seize territory and to subjugate the local population as well as its attempts of local governance indicate that $r_{AQ} \leq r_D$ holds as *Daesh* may benefit more from small-scale attacks due to its local alignment than *al-Qaeda*.

From a purely technical point of view, the costs associated with a small-scale incident should not differ much between the two movements. However, *Daesh* has shown to engage in behavior that leads to quick results by intimidating and committing simple but nasty attacks. Since *al-Qaeda* tries to capitalize on *Daesh*'s brutality and portrays itself as a more moderate actor, it is plausible to assume that small-scale attacks can be more expensive for *al-Qaeda* than for *Daesh* due to the potential reputational costs for *al-Qaeda*, that is, $c_{AQ} \geq c_D$ is assumed to hold.

Furthermore, because *al-Qaeda* is a globally operating network that has gained experience and has proved to be innovative,[2] it is reasonable to assume that *al-Qaeda* has greater capabilities than *Daesh* to accomplish a large-scale event, which is expected to result in lower costs associated with a spectacular attack for al-Qaeda, that is, $C_{IS} > C_{AQ}$. Nevertheless, it is still assumed that the payoff of a large-scale attack exceeds that of a small-scale attack.

Then

$$R_{AQ} - C_{AQ} > R_D - C_D \tag{6.2}$$

and

$$r_{AQ} - c_{AQ} < r_D - c_D \tag{6.3}$$

hold true, when analyzing the alleged asymmetry between *al-Qaeda* and *Daesh*.

---

[2] 9/11 has been an example of innovation on the part of the terrorists because it combined two approaches that were each used before, airplane hijacking and suicide bombing, but were never combined in this form. A second example of innovation is the use of IEDs in Afghanistan and Iraq (Intriligator 2010, p. 4).

Following the reasoning for *al-Qaeda*'s global alignment, it is conceivable to imagine that the rewards associated with a large-scale attack vastly exceed those of a small-scale attack, so that *al-Qaeda* might have a dominant strategy for (*wait*, *large*), or if not, at least will favor a Nash-equilibrium, in which it commits a large-scale incident, meaning that

$$2r_{AQ} - 2c_{AQ} < R_{AQ} - C_{AQ} \tag{6.4}$$

applies.

Contrary, *Daesh*'s focus on local governance would imply

$$2r_D - 2c_D > R_D - C_D. \tag{6.5}$$

Regardless of whether *al-Qaeda* does have or does not have a dominant strategy, the Nash-equilibrium [*small*, *small*; *wait*, *large*] will be played, even if the game has multiple Nash-equilibria.

However, the result is merely caused by the assumption of different alignments. Further, the setbacks *Daesh* has had since gaining momentum in 2014 and continues to experience, has shown that an orientation towards local governance is not a sustainable model, particularly, when taking into account the effects of competition between *Daesh* and *Jabhat Fateh al-Sham* on their attack behavior.

Daesh's reliance on foreign fighters facilitates the change from a local to a global oriented terror group. From 2012 to 2015, individuals from Central Asia and Europe, have been mobilized in unprecedented numbers to join the ranks of *Daesh* (Soufan Group Report 2017). Accordingly, a major challenge will be the ability, among others, of the remaining foreign *Daesh* members to carry out terrorist attacks.

Given *Daesh*'s shift toward a global oriented terror group, matching the different strategies occurring in Western countries is the more appropriate scenario, when analyzing the rivalry of *al-Qaeda* and *Daesh*. This simply accounts for the risk imposed by returning foreign fighters—and more importantly, when it comes to the effects of competition between the two movements—terrorist incidents in Western countries serve as a signal to potential supporters to join the ranks of a terrorist organization, which may particularly serve *Daesh* as a means for procurement and replenishment in order to hold, expand, and defeat (local) caliphates in a phase of repression.

Figure 6.2, then, shows the game relating to the situation described.

Then, the solution to the game depends on

$$2r_D - 2c_D \gtrless \frac{1}{2}R_D - C_D. \tag{6.6}$$

If and only if $R_D \gg r_D$, or $\frac{1}{4}R_D > r_D$ in model terms, holds, *Daesh* may favor a large-scale attack over two small events, depending on the relation of the costs and rewards margins. Otherwise, *Daesh* will prefer to carry out two small-scale attacks.

Relaxing $R_{AQ} \gg r_{AQ}$ and assuming $4r_{AQ} > R_{AQ} > 2r_{AQ}$ inevitably will result in multiple as has been shown in Sect. 5.1. However, if *al-Qaeda* prefers one

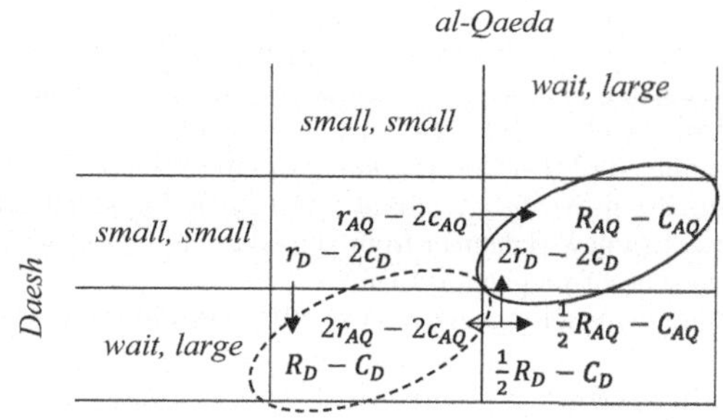

Fig. 6.2 *Al-Qaeda* Versus *Daesh*. Note: Since it is not necessarily the case that *al-Qaeda* has a dominant strategy, the game can result in multiple Nash-equilibria (the second equilibrium in pure strategies is depicted in dashed line). However, the analysis explains why the Nash-equilibrium in the right-hand cell will be played

spectacular event over two small-scale attacks, i.e., (Eq. 6.4) is still valid, which, given the preferences of *al-Qaeda*, appears likely to hold more than not, and *Daesh* favors to small-scale attacks over a large-scale attack, then [*small, small*; *wait, large*] is the plausible solution despite the existence of other Nash-equilibria.

A further explanation for the plausibility of [*small, small*; *wait, large*] is *al-Qaeda*'s credibility concerning its ability to commit a large-scale attack. The fact that *al-Qaeda* has proven to be capable of carrying out 9/11 in the past may force *Daesh*, even if it also favors a spectacular attack, to conduct two small-scale attacks from the very beginning as *Daesh* may expect to lose when participating in a race for a large-scale attack.

The case study of *al-Qaeda* and *Daesh* provides an example of how reputation can affect the attack behavior in a competitive environment: *al-Qaeda*'s reputation curbs *Daesh* and explains the occurrence of recent attacks in Berlin, Nice, or Strasbourg, which are considered to be of a small-scale attack type.

However, it can also be deemed that *Daesh* will try to commit a large-scale attack sooner or later if the effect of *al-Qaeda*'s reputation will abate because, as Sect. 5.3 has shown, for $2_D - 2c_D < R_D - C_D$ it is always better to participate in the race as long as sunk costs of preparing a large-scale attack are sufficiently small.

References

Al-Adnani SAM (2011) The state of Islam will remain safe. Al-Furqan Media. Accessed October 06, 2018. https://scholarship.tricolib.brynmawr.edu/bitstream/handle/10066/15267/ADN20110807.pdf?sequence=1

Al-Adnani SAM (2014) Sorry Amir of al-Qaeda. Al-Furqan Media. Accessed 6 Oct 2018. https://azelin.files.wordpress.com/2014/05/shaykh-abc5ab-mue1b8a5ammad-al-e28098adnc481nc4ab-al-shc481mc4ab-22sorry-amc4abr-of-al-qc481_idah22-en1.pdf

Al-Baghdadi SAB (2013) Announcement of the Islamic State of Iraq and al-Sham. al-Furqan Media. Accessed 7 Oct 2018. https://jihadology.net/2013/04/09/al-furqan-media-presents-a-new-audio-message-from-the-islamic-state-of-iraqs-shaykh-abu-bakr-al-ḥussayni-al-qurayshi-al-baghdadi-announcement-of-the-islamic-state-of-iraq-an/

Al-Julani AM (2013) About the fields of al-Sham. al-Manarah al-Bayda Foundation for Media Production. Accessed 9 Oct 2018. https://jihadology.net/2013/04/10/al-manarah-al-bayḍa-foundation-for-media-production-presents-a-new-audio-message-from-jabhat-al-nuṣrahs-abu-muḥammad-al-jawlani-al-golani-about-the-fields-of-al-sham/
Al-Qaeda's General Command (2014) On the relationship of Qaidat al-Jihad and the Islamic State of Iraq and al-Sham. al-Fajr Media. Accessed 7 Oct 2018. https://jihadology.net/2014/02/02/as-saḥab-media-presents-a-new-statement-from-al-qaidah-on-the-relationship-of-qaidat-al-jihad-and-the-islamic-state-of-iraq-and-al-sham/
Al-Zawahiri A (2005) Untitled letter. Accessed 5 Oct 2018. https://fas.org/irp/news/2005/10/letter_in_english.pdf
Al-Zawahiri A (2008) The open meeting with Shaykh Ayman al-Zawahiri. Accessed 10 Oct 2018. http://www.washingtonpost.com/wp-srv/world/OpenMeetingZawahiri_Part1.pdf
Al-Zawahiri A (2013) General guidelines for the work of a Jihadi. As-Sahab Media. Accessed 13 Oct 2018. https://azelin.files.wordpress.com/2013/09/dr-ayman-al-e1ba93awc481hirc4ab-22general-guidelines-for-the-work-of-a-jihc481dc4ab22-en.pdf
Al-Zawahiri A (2014) Testimony to preserve the blood of the Mujahidin in al-Sham. As-Sahab Media. Accessed 6 Oct 2018. https://azelin.files.wordpress.com/2014/05/dr-ayman-al-e1ba93awc481hirc4ab-22testimony-to-preserve-the-blood-of-the-mujc481hidc4abn-in-al-shc481m22-en.pdf
Brownstein R, Wright R (2001) Bin Laden's goals seemingly elusive. Chicago Tribune. Accessed 12 Dec 2018. www.chicagotribune.com/news/nationworld/sns-worldtrade-binladen-lat-story.html
Crider JR (2009) A view from inside the surge. Mil Rev 89(2):81–88
Dabiq (2014) The return of the Kilafah. Accessed 13 Oct 2018. https://clarionproject.org/docs/isis-isil-islamic-state-magazine-Issue-1-the-return-of-khilafah.pdf
Fishman B (2009) Dysfunction and decline: lessons learned from inside Al-Qaida in Iraq. In: Harmony Project. Combating Terrorism Center, West Point, NY
Hassan H, Barabandi B (2016) Al-Qaeda steps back to let nusra move forward in Syria. Tahrir Institute for Middle East Policy. Accessed 12 Oct 2018. https://timep.org/c ommentary/analysis/al-qaeda-steps-back-to-let-nusra-move-forward-in-syria/
Intriligator MD (2010) The economics of terrorism. Econ Inq 48(1):1–13
Johnston PB, Shapiro JN, Shatz HJ, Bahney B, Jung DF, Ryan P, Wallace J (2016) Foundations of the Islamic State: management, money, and terror in Iraq, 2005–2010. RAND Corporation, Santa Monica, CA
McCants W (2013) How Zawahiri Lost al Qaeda. Foreign Affairs. http://www.foreignaffairs.com/articles/140273/william-mccants/how-zawahiri-lost-al-qaeda
Mortada R (2014) Al-Qaeda(s) in Syria: from foundation to fracture. Al Akhbar
Rabasa A, Chalk P, Cragin K, Daly SA, Gregg HS, Karasik TW, O'Brien KA, Rosenau W (2006) Beyond al-Qaeda. Part 1. The global jihadist movement. RAND Corporation, Santa Monica, CA
Roggio B (2013) Suicide bombers kill 14 in Damascus. Longwarjournal. Accessed 12 Dec 2018. https://www.longwarjournal.org/archives/2013/06/suicide_bombers_kill_14_in_dam.php
Saltman EM, Winter C (2014) Islamic state: the changing face of modern Jihadism. Quilliam Foundation, London
Soufan Group Report (2017) Beyond the caliphate: foreign fighters and the threat of returnees. The Soufan Center
Wagemakers J (2011) Protecting Jihad: The Sharia Council of the Minbar al-Tawhid wa-l-Jihad. Middle East Policy 18(2):148–162
Whitlock C (2004) Grisly path to power in Iraq's insurgency. Washington Post. Accessed 4 Oct 2018. http://www.washingtonpost.com/wp-dyn/content/article/2004/09/27/AR2005040209346.html
Yusufzai R (2001) Face to face with Osama. The Guardian. Accessed 12 Dec 2018. https://www.theguardian.com/world/2001/sep/26/afghanistan.terrorism3
Zelin AY (2014) The war between ISIS and al-Qaeda for supremacy of the global jihadist movement. Wash Inst Near East Policy 20(1):1–11

Chapter 7
Conclusion

Abstract A major concern of terrorist groups is to ensure sustainability and longevity. By committing attacks of varying degrees, terrorists can attract resources, which enable an organization to improve its chances of achieving stated goals. However, support is assumed to be provided to the most capable group, implying that terrorist groups are incentivized to signal their capabilities. This is where the outbidding hypothesis developed by Bloom (2004) draws on. In an environment, where several terrorist organizations are competing for a given supportive mass, terrorists are supposed to increase their activities, either quantitatively or qualitatively. Although Bloom's idea is intuitively appealing, it is merely supported by anecdotical and few empirical evidence.

A major concern of terrorist groups is to ensure sustainability and longevity. By committing attacks of varying degrees, terrorists can attract resources, which enable an organization to improve its chances of achieving stated goals. However, support is assumed to be provided to the most capable group, implying that terrorist groups are incentivized to signal their capabilities. This is where the outbidding hypothesis developed by Bloom (2004) draws on. In an environment, where several terrorist organizations are competing for a given supportive mass, terrorists are supposed to increase their activities, either quantitatively or qualitatively. Although Bloom's idea is intuitively appealing, it is merely supported by anecdotical and few empirical evidence.

Game theory is a useful concept to analyze situations, in which actors make decisions that are interdependent, and has become an important framework in the study of terrorism. Therefore, game theory is an appropriate tool, when it comes to the question of how competition may affect terrorist group behavior. However, attempts to apply game theory to terrorism research mainly focused on interactions between governments in the context of counterterrorism or between governments and terror groups.

The purpose of this thesis has been the systematic analysis of the effects of competition on terrorist groups, which vie for supremacy. To this end, a game-theoretical model was developed, which examines the interdependency of two

© The Author(s), under exclusive license to Springer Nature Switzerland AG 2020
N. Ismael, *Strategic Interaction Between Islamist Terror Groups*, SpringerBriefs in Economics, https://doi.org/10.1007/978-3-030-51307-8_7

terrorist organizations that can commit a large-scale attack or carry out maximally two small-scale attacks.

The analysis shows that competition between terrorist groups can be interpreted as a race for which group can play its preferred strategy first. The findings suggest that, if groups prefer two small-scale attacks over a large-scale event, the player that can carry out a small-scale attack first compels the other to commit a large-scale attack, providing an explanation for why large-scale attacks occur at all. Applying the model to the alleged rivalry between *Daesh* and the unofficial al-Qaeda branch Jabhat Fateh al-Sham reveals that *Daesh*'s shift toward committing attacks in the West may be, among others, the result of a lost race for two small-scale attacks.

In case of multiple Nash-equilibria with a preference for conducting a large-scale attack, the analysis shows that terror organizations have a dominant strategy to participate in a race for conducting a large-scale attack, though risk losing if the sunk costs associated with preparing a spectacular event are sufficiently small, which has been suggested to hold.

When applying the model to al-Qaeda and *Daesh*, it is argued that *Daesh*'s decision about the scale of an attack is affected by the past 9/11 successes of al-Qaeda. If *Daesh* assumes to lose the contest because al-Qaeda has proven to be capable of conducting a large-scale attack in the past, *Daesh* would be better off by carrying out two small-scale attacks, explaining why *Daesh* has not committed a 9/11-like attack yet but more mundane attacks such as Berlin, Nice, or Strasbourg.

In general, the interpretation of competition between terror groups as a race exhibits that a competitive environment does not necessarily lead to more attacks but can result in less terrorism due to an increased probability of attack failure induced by the race. This is different from the idea of outbidding, which attributes a reduction of terrorism to a decline in the acceptance of terrorist violence within the followership.

Terrorist behavior remains puzzling. However, theorizing the interplay of terror organizations can help to understand how groups' decision-making is affected by rivalry beyond the scope of decreased acceptance among the supportive mass and increased efforts of counterterrorism. Even if there are any concerns regarding a systematic pattern of attack, terrorist groups may play a mixed strategy, so that the occurrence of attacks appear to be random to an outsider.

Reference

Bloom MM (2004) Palestinian suicide bombing: Public support, market share, and outbidding. Political Science Quarterly 119(1):61–88

Appendix A

Let group A be the player, who mixes with probabilities p_i and group B with probabilities q_i. Then, the p-mix for group A consisting of using (*small, wait*), (*wait, small*), (*small, small*), (*wait, large*) and (*wait, wait*) is determined in proportions p_1, p_2, p_3, p_4, and p_5, and the q-mix for group B in proportions q_1, q_2, q_3, q_4, and q_5, respectively.[1]

The p- and q-mix must separately satisfy the conditions of probabilities, i.e., $\sum_i^n p_i = 1$ and $\sum_i^n q_i = 1$ with $p_i \geq 0$ and $q_i \geq 0$, respectively, and constitute a situation from which the player does not want to deviate (Nash 1951, p. 286f.).

The expected payoffs, exemplified for group A, are

$$\begin{aligned} E(small, wait) &= E(\theta_1) \\ &= q_1\left(\frac{1}{2}r - c\right) + q_2(r - c) + q_3\left(\frac{1}{2}r - c\right) \\ &\quad + (1 - q_1 - q_2 - q_3 - q_5)(r - c) + q_5(r - c) \\ &= r - c - \frac{1}{2}rq_1 - \frac{1}{2}rq_3 \end{aligned}$$

[1]Note that in $n \times xn$-games with $n > 2$ simply considering the actions constituting pure-strategy equilibria does not necessarily lead to the correct mixed-strategy equilibrium as some actions, though played in a pure-strategy equilibrium, may be unused in a mix or, conversely, actions are used in the mix, although not part of a pure-strategy equilibrium. For a numerical example see Bernheim (1984).

© The Author(s), under exclusive license to Springer Nature Switzerland AG 2020

N. Ismael, *Strategic Interaction Between Islamist Terror Groups*, SpringerBriefs in Economics, https://doi.org/10.1007/978-3-030-51307-8

$$
\begin{aligned}
E(wait, small) &= E(\theta_2)\\
&= q_1(r-c) + q_2\left(\frac{1}{2}r - c\right) + q_3\left(\frac{1}{2}r - c\right)\\
&\quad + (1 - q_1 - q_2 - q_3 - q_5)(r-c) + q_5(r-c)\\
&= r - c - \frac{1}{2}rq_2 - \frac{1}{2}rq_3
\end{aligned}
$$

$$
\begin{aligned}
E(small, small) &= E(\theta_3)\\
&= q_1\left(\frac{3}{2}r - 2c\right) + q_2\left(\frac{3}{2}r - 2c\right) + q_3(r - 2c)\\
&\quad + (1 - q_1 - q_2 - q_3 - q_5)(2r - 2c) + q_5(2r - 2c)\\
&= 2r - 2c - \frac{1}{2}rq_1 - \frac{1}{2}rq_2 - rq_3
\end{aligned}
$$

$$
\begin{aligned}
E(wait, large) &= E(\theta_4)\\
&= q_1(R - C) + q_2(R - C) + q_3(R - C) + (1 - q_1 - q_2 - q_3 - q_5)\\
&\quad \times \left(\frac{1}{2}R - C\right) + q_5(R - C)\\
&= \frac{1}{2}R - C + \frac{1}{2}Rq_1 + \frac{1}{2}Rq_2 + \frac{1}{2}Rq_3 + \frac{1}{2}Rq_5
\end{aligned}
$$

$$
E(wait, wait) = E(\theta_5) = 0
$$

Due to symmetry, the expected payoffs for group B are equivalent.

To ascertain the set of mixed-strategy Nash equilibria, the so-called indifference principle is used: a profile of mixed strategies is a Nash equilibrium if and only if for each player all definite strategies realizable under a certain mixed strategy yield the same expected payoff for a player, and all definite strategies not realizable under a certain mixed strategy yield an expected payoff for a player that does not exceed that of definite strategies realizable under a certain mixed strategy.

Further, a mixed strategy that assigns a positive probability to a dominated pure strategy is dominated and, therefore, has an incentive to deviate (Nash 1951, p. 292). As argued in Sect. 5.1 (*wait, wait*), (*small, wait*), and (*wait, small*) are strictly dominated. Hence, these strategies are not considered, i.e., $q_1^* = q_2^* = q_5^* = 0$, as every player has an incentive to deviate from the mix that contains one of the three strategies.

Then

$$E(\theta_3) = 2r - 2c - rq_3 = \frac{1}{2}R - C + \frac{1}{2}Rq_3 = E(\theta_4)$$

yields

$$q_3^* = \frac{2r - 2c - \left(\frac{1}{2}R - C\right)}{\frac{1}{2}R + r}$$

so that

$$q_4^* = 1 - \frac{2r - 2c - \left(\frac{1}{2}R - C\right)}{\frac{1}{2}R + r} = \frac{R - C - (r - 2c)}{\frac{1}{2}R + r}.$$

In the only mixed-strategy equilibrium, each group mixes on two of five strategies, namely (*small, small*) and (*wait, large*), with weights $\left(0, 0, \frac{2r-2c-\left(\frac{1}{2}R-C\right)}{\frac{1}{2}R+r}, \frac{R-C-(r-2c)}{\frac{1}{2}R+r}, 0\right)$.

Appendix B

Again, group A mixes with probabilities p_i and group B with probabilities q_i. Due to the changed payoff for the strategy (*wait, large*), which must be interpreted as participating in the race and playing small during period two, when losing, now

$$
\begin{aligned}
E(wait, large) &= E(\theta_4) \\
&= q_1(R-C) + q_2(R-C) + q_3(R-C) + (1-q_1-q_2-q_3-q_5) \\
&\quad \times \left[\frac{1}{2}(r-c-FC) + \frac{1}{2}(R-C)\right] + q_5(R-C)
\end{aligned}
$$

holds.

Despite the adjustment, (*wait, small*), (*small, wait*), and (*wait, wait*) are still dominated, so that $q_1^* = q_2^* = q_5^* = 0$.

Thus, both $E(\theta_3)$ and $E(\theta_4)$ can be simplified to

$$E(\theta_3) = q_3(r-2c) + (1-q_3)(2r-2c)$$

and

$$E(\theta_4) = q_3(R-C) + (1-q_3)\left[\frac{1}{2}(r-c-FC) + \frac{1}{2}(R-C)\right].$$

Then,

$$
\begin{aligned}
E(\theta_3) &= q_3(r-2c) \\
&\quad + \left(1-q_3\right)(2r-2c) = q_3(R-C) + (1-q_3)\left[\frac{1}{2}(r-c-FC) + \frac{1}{2}(R-C)\right] = E(\theta_4)
\end{aligned}
$$

leads to

© The Author(s), under exclusive license to Springer Nature Switzerland AG 2020

N. Ismael, *Strategic Interaction Between Islamist Terror Groups*, SpringerBriefs in Economics, https://doi.org/10.1007/978-3-030-51307-8

$$q_3^* = \frac{3(r-c) - (R-C) + FC}{r+c+R-C+FC}$$

and

$$q_4^* = 1 - q_3^* = 1 - \frac{3(r-c) - (R-C) + FC}{r+c+R-C+FC} = \frac{2(R-C) - 2(r-2c)}{r+c+R-C+FC}.$$

The mixed strategy-equilibrium for each player contains (*small, small*) and (*wait, large*) with weights $\left(0, 0, \frac{3(r-c)-(R-C)+FC}{r+c+R-C+FC}, \frac{2(R-C)-2(r-2c)}{r+c+R-C+FC}, 0\right)$.

References

Bernheim BD (1984) Rationalizable strategic behavior. Econometrica 52(4):1007–1028
Nash J (1951) Non-cooperative games. Ann Math 54(2):286–295

© The Author(s), under exclusive license to Springer Nature Switzerland AG 2020

N. Ismael, *Strategic Interaction Between Islamist Terror Groups*, SpringerBriefs in Economics, https://doi.org/10.1007/978-3-030-51307-8